FAVORITE BRAND NAME
COOKIES & BROWNIES

Publications International, Ltd.

Microwave Cooking: Microwave ovens vary in wattage. The
microwave cooking times given in this publication are approximate.
Use the cooking times as guidelines and check for doneness before
adding more time. Consult manufacturer's instructions for suitable
microwave-safe cooking dishes.

FAVORITE BRAND NAME
COOKIES & BROWNIES

 Chock-Full

O' CHIPS

Oatmeal Scotchies

1¼ cups all-purpose flour
1 teaspoon baking soda
½ teaspoon salt
½ teaspoon ground cinnamon
1 cup (2 sticks) butter or margarine,
     softened
¾ cup granulated sugar
¾ cup packed brown sugar
2 eggs
1 teaspoon vanilla extract or grated peel
     of 1 orange
3 cups quick or old-fashioned oats
1⅔ cups (11-ounce package) NESTLÉ®
     TOLL HOUSE® Butterscotch
     Flavored Morsels

COMBINE flour, baking soda, salt and cinnamon in small bowl. Beat butter, granulated sugar, brown sugar, eggs and vanilla in large mixer bowl. Gradually beat in flour mixture. Stir in oats and morsels. Drop by rounded tablespoon onto ungreased baking sheets.

BAKE in preheated 375°F. oven for 7 to 8 minutes for chewy cookies; 9 to 10 minutes for crisp cookies. Cool on baking sheets for 2 minutes; remove to wire racks to cool completely.   *Makes about 4 dozen cookies*

Pan Cookie Variation: Prepare dough as above. Spread dough into greased 15½×10½-inch jelly-roll pan. Bake in preheated 375°F. oven for 18 to 22 minutes or until very lightly browned. Cool completely on wire rack. Makes 4 dozen bars.

Orange-Walnut Chippers

½ cup butter or margarine, softened
1 cup packed light brown sugar
1 egg
1 tablespoon grated orange peel
½ cup all-purpose flour
¼ teaspoon baking soda
¼ teaspoon salt
1½ cups uncooked rolled oats
1 cup semisweet chocolate chips
½ cup coarsely chopped walnuts

1. Preheat oven to 375°F. Lightly grease cookie sheets.

2. Beat butter and sugar in large bowl until light and fluffy. Beat in egg and orange peel. Add flour, baking soda and salt to butter mixture. Beat until well blended. Stir in oats, chips and nuts. Drop by rounded teaspoonfuls 2 inches apart onto prepared cookie sheets.

3. Bake 10 to 12 minutes until golden brown. Let cookies stand on cookie sheets 2 minutes. Remove cookies to wire racks; cool completely. Store tightly covered.   *Makes about 3 dozen cookies*

Giant Raisin-Chip Frisbees

1 **cup butter or margarine, softened**
1 **cup packed brown sugar**
½ **cup granulated sugar**
2 **eggs**
1 **teaspoon vanilla extract**
1½ **cups all-purpose flour**
¼ **cup unsweetened cocoa powder**
1 **teaspoon baking soda**
1 **cup (6 ounces) semisweet chocolate chips**
¾ **cup raisins**
¾ **cup chopped walnuts**

1. Preheat oven to 350°F. Line cookie sheets with parchment paper or lightly grease and dust with flour.

2. Beat butter and both sugars in large bowl. Add eggs and vanilla; beat until light. Combine flour, cocoa and baking soda in small bowl. Add to butter mixture with chocolate chips, raisins and walnuts; stir until well blended.

3. Scoop out about ½ cup of dough for each cookie. Place on prepared cookie sheets, spacing about 5 inches apart. Using knife dipped in water, smooth balls of dough out to about 3½ inches in diameter. Bake 10 to 12 minutes until golden. Remove to wire racks; cool completely. Store tightly covered.

Makes about 16 cookies

Cowboy Cookies

½ cup butter or margarine, softened
½ cup packed light brown sugar
¼ cup granulated sugar
1 egg
1 teaspoon vanilla extract
1 cup all-purpose flour
2 tablespoons unsweetened cocoa powder
½ teaspoon baking powder
¼ teaspoon baking soda
1 cup uncooked rolled oats
1 cup (6 ounces) semisweet chocolate
    chips
½ cup raisins
½ cup chopped nuts

1. Preheat oven to 375°F. Lightly grease cookie sheets or line with parchment paper.

2. Beat butter with sugars in large bowl until blended. Add egg and vanilla; beat until fluffy. Combine flour, cocoa, baking powder and baking soda in small bowl; stir into butter mixture. Add oats, chocolate chips, raisins and nuts. Drop by rounded teaspoonfuls 2 inches apart onto prepared cookie sheets.

3. Bake 10 to 12 minutes until lightly browned around edges. Remove to wire racks; cool completely. Store tightly covered.   *Makes about 4 dozen cookies*

Chocolate Chip Chewies

1¼ cups firmly packed light brown sugar
¾ BUTTER FLAVOR* CRISCO® Stick or
    ¾ cup BUTTER FLAVOR CRISCO
    all-vegetable shortening
2 tablespoons milk
1 tablespoon vanilla
1 egg
1¾ cups all-purpose flour
1 teaspoon salt
¾ teaspoon baking soda
1 cup coarsely chopped pecans
1 cup quick oats, uncooked
1 cup semisweet chocolate chips
⅓ cup flake coconut

1. Heat oven to 375°F. **Place** sheets of foil on countertop for cooling cookies.

2. Combine brown sugar, shortening, milk and vanilla in large bowl. **Beat** at medium speed of electric mixer until well blended. **Beat** egg into shortening mixture.

3. Combine flour, salt and baking soda. **Mix** into shortening mixture just until blended. **Stir** in pecans, oats, chocolate chips and coconut.

4. Drop by rounded measuring tablespoonfuls of dough 3 inches apart onto ungreased baking sheets.

5. Bake one baking sheet at a time at 375°F for 8 to 10 minutes for chewy cookies (11 to 13 minutes for crisp cookies). *Do not overbake.* **Cool** 2 minutes. **Remove** to foil; cool completely.   *Makes 4 dozen cookies*

*Butter Flavor Crisco is artificially flavored.

Whole-Grain Chippers

1 cup butter or margarine, softened
⅔ cup granulated sugar
1 cup packed light brown sugar
2 eggs
1 teaspoon baking soda
1 teaspoon vanilla extract
  Pinch salt
1 cup whole wheat flour
1 cup all-purpose flour
2 cups uncooked rolled oats
1 package (12 ounces) semisweet
  chocolate chips
1 cup sunflower seeds

1. Preheat oven to 375°F. Lightly grease cookie sheets or line with parchment paper.

2. Beat butter, sugars and eggs in large bowl until light and fluffy. Beat in baking soda, vanilla and salt. Blend in flours and oats to make a stiff dough. Stir in chocolate chips. Shape rounded teaspoonfuls of dough into balls; roll in sunflower seeds. Place 2 inches apart on prepared cookie sheets.

3. Bake 8 to 10 minutes until firm. *Do not overbake.* Cool a few minutes on cookie sheets, then remove to wire racks; cool completely. Store tightly covered.

Makes about 6 dozen cookies

Chocolate Oatmeal Chippers

1¼ cups all-purpose flour
½ cup NESTLÉ® TOLL HOUSE® Baking Cocoa
1 teaspoon baking soda
¼ teaspoon salt
1 cup (2 sticks) butter or margarine, softened
1 cup packed brown sugar
½ cup granulated sugar
1 teaspoon vanilla extract
2 eggs
2 cups (11.5-ounce package) NESTLÉ® TOLL HOUSE® Milk Chocolate Morsels
1¾ cups quick or old-fashioned oats
1 cup chopped nuts (optional)

COMBINE flour, cocoa, baking soda and salt in medium bowl. Beat butter, brown sugar, granulated sugar and vanilla in large mixer bowl until creamy. Beat in eggs. Gradually beat in flour mixture. Stir in morsels, oats and nuts. Drop by rounded tablespoon onto ungreased baking sheets.

BAKE in preheated 375°F. oven for 9 to 12 minutes or until edges are set but centers are still soft. Cool on baking sheets for 2 minutes; remove to wire racks to cool completely. *Makes about 4 dozen cookies*

Oatmeal Brownie Drops

- ½ cup (1 stick) butter or margarine, softened
- ¾ cup sugar
- 2 eggs
- 1 teaspoon vanilla extract
- 1 cup all-purpose flour
- ½ cup HERSHEY'S Cocoa
- ¼ teaspoon baking soda
- 1 cup quick-cooking rolled oats
- 1 cup HERSHEY'S MINI CHIPS® Semi-Sweet Chocolate

Heat oven to 350°F. In large bowl, beat together butter and sugar until creamy. Add eggs and vanilla; beat well. Stir together flour, cocoa and baking soda; gradually add to butter mixture, blending thoroughly. Stir in oats and small chocolate chips. Drop dough by tablespoons onto ungreased cookie sheet. Bake 7 to 8 minutes or until cookies begin to set. *Do not overbake.* Remove from cookie sheet to wire rack. Cool completely. *Makes about 3½ dozen cookies*

Cherry Cashew Cookies

1   cup butter or margarine, softened
¾   cup granulated sugar
¾   cup packed brown sugar
1   teaspoon vanilla extract
2   eggs
2¼   cups all-purpose flour
1   teaspoon baking soda
1   package (10 ounces) vanilla milk chips
        (about 1⅔ cups)
1   cup broken, salted cashews
1½   cups dried tart cherries

Preheat oven to 375°F.

In large mixer bowl, combine butter, granulated sugar,
brown sugar, vanilla and eggs. Mix with electric mixer
on medium speed until thoroughly combined.
Combine flour and baking soda; gradually stir flour
mixture into butter mixture. Stir in vanilla milk chips,
cashews and dried cherries. Drop by rounded
tablespoonfuls onto ungreased baking sheets.

Bake 12 to 15 minutes or until light golden brown.
Cool on wire racks and store in airtight container.

Makes 4½ dozen cookies

Favorite recipe from **Cherry Marketing Institute, Inc.**

Cherry Chocolate Chip Walnut Cookies

  1 **cup sugar**
  ¼ **cup Prune Purée (page 280) or prepared prune butter *or* 1 jar (2½ ounces) first-stage baby food prunes**
  ¼ **cup water**
  2 **tablespoons nonfat milk**
  1 **teaspoon vanilla**
  ½ **teaspoon instant espresso coffee powder *or* 1 teaspoon instant coffee**
  1 **cup all-purpose flour**
  ½ **cup unsweetened cocoa powder**
  ¾ **teaspoon baking soda**
  ½ **teaspoon salt**
  ½ **cup dried sour cherries**
  ¼ **cup chopped walnuts**
  ¼ **cup semisweet chocolate chips**

Preheat oven to 350°F. Coat baking sheets with vegetable cooking spray. In large bowl, whisk together sugar, prune purée, water, milk, vanilla and espresso powder until mixture is well blended, about 1 minute. Combine flour, cocoa, baking soda and salt; mix into prune purée mixture until well blended. Stir in cherries, walnuts and chocolate chips. Spoon twelve equal mounds of dough onto prepared baking sheets, spacing at least 2 inches apart. Bake in center of oven 18 to 20 minutes or until set and tops of cookies feel dry to the touch. Cool on baking sheets 2 minutes; remove to wire rack to cool completely.

Makes 12 large cookies

Favorite recipe from **California Prune Board**

Chewy Brownie Cookies

1½ cups firmly packed light brown sugar
⅔ CRISCO® Stick or ⅔ cup CRISCO all-vegetable shortening
1 tablespoon water
1 teaspoon vanilla
2 eggs
1½ cups all-purpose flour
⅓ cup unsweetened baking cocoa
¼ teaspoon baking soda
½ teaspoon salt
2 cups semi-sweet chocolate chips (12-ounce package)

1. Heat oven to 375°F. **Place** sheets of foil on countertop for cooling cookies.

2. Combine brown sugar, shortening, water and vanilla in large bowl. **Beat** at medium speed of electric mixer until well blended. **Beat** eggs into creamed mixture.

3. Combine flour, cocoa, baking soda and salt. **Mix** into creamed mixture at low speed just until blended. **Stir** in chocolate chips.

4. Drop rounded measuring tablespoonfuls of dough 2 inches apart onto ungreased baking sheet.

5. Bake one baking sheet at a time at 375°F for 7 to 9 minutes, or until cookies are set. *Do not overbake.* **Cool** 2 minutes on baking sheet. **Remove** cookies to foil to cool completely.

Makes about 3 dozen cookies

White Chocolate Biggies

1½ cups butter or margarine, softened
1 cup granulated sugar
¾ cup packed light brown sugar
2 teaspoons vanilla extract
2 eggs
2½ cups all-purpose flour
⅔ cup unsweetened cocoa powder
1 teaspoon baking soda
½ teaspoon salt
1 package (10 ounces) large white chocolate chips *or* 1 white chocolate bar, cut into pieces
¾ cup pecan halves, coarsely chopped
½ cup golden raisins

1. Preheat oven to 350°F. Lightly grease cookie sheets or line with parchment paper.

2. Beat butter, sugars, vanilla and eggs in large bowl until light and fluffy. Combine flour, cocoa, baking soda and salt in medium bowl; blend into butter mixture until smooth. Stir in white chocolate chips, pecans and raisins.

3. Scoop out about ⅓ cupful of dough for each cookie. Place on prepared cookie sheets, spacing about 4 inches apart. Press each cookie to flatten slightly.

4. Bake 12 to 14 minutes until firm in center. Cool 5 minutes on cookie sheets, then remove to wire racks; cool completely. Store tightly covered.

Makes about 2 dozen cookies

HERSHEY®'S White Chip Chocolate Cookies

- 1 cup (2 sticks) butter or margarine, softened
- 2 cups sugar
- 2 eggs
- 2 teaspoons vanilla extract
- 2 cups all-purpose flour
- ¾ cup HERSHEY®'S Cocoa
- 1 teaspoon baking soda
- ½ teaspoon salt
- 1⅔ cups (10-ounce package) HERSHEY®'S Premier White Chips

Heat oven to 350°F. In large bowl, beat butter and sugar until creamy. Add eggs and vanilla; beat until light and fluffy. Stir together flour, cocoa, baking soda and salt; gradually blend into butter mixture. Stir in white chips. Drop by rounded teaspoons onto ungreased cookie sheets.

Bake 8 to 9 minutes. (Do not overbake, cookies will be soft. They will puff while baking; flatten upon cooling.) Cool slightly; remove from cookie sheets to wire racks. Cool completely.   *Makes about 4½ dozen cookies*

Ultimate Chippers

2½ cups all-purpose flour
1 teaspoon baking soda
½ teaspoon salt
1 cup butter or margarine, softened
1 cup packed light brown sugar
½ cup granulated sugar
2 eggs
1 tablespoon vanilla extract
1 cup semisweet chocolate chips
1 cup milk chocolate chips
1 cup vanilla milk chips
½ cup coarsely chopped pecans (optional)

1. Preheat oven to 375°F.

2. Combine flour, baking soda and salt in medium bowl. Beat butter, brown sugar and granulated sugar in large bowl until light and fluffy. Beat in eggs and vanilla. Add flour mixture to butter mixture; beat until well blended. Stir in chips and pecans.

3. Drop by heaping teaspoonfuls 2 inches apart onto ungreased cookie sheets. Bake 10 to 12 minutes until edges are golden brown. Let cookies stand on cookie sheets 2 minutes. Remove cookies to wire racks; cool completely. Store tightly covered.

Makes about 6 dozen cookies

Symphony Milk Chocolate Macadamia Cookies

1   HERSHEY'S SYMPHONY® Milk
    Chocolate Bar or Milk Chocolate Bar
    with Almonds & Toffee Chips
    (7 ounces)
6   tablespoons butter or margarine,
    softened
½   cup granulated sugar
¼   cup packed light brown sugar
½   teaspoon vanilla extract
1   egg
1   cup all-purpose flour
½   teaspoon baking soda
1   cup coarsely chopped macadamia nuts

Heat oven to 350°F. Cut chocolate bar into ¼-inch
pieces. In large bowl, beat butter, granulated sugar,
brown sugar and vanilla until creamy. Add egg; beat
well. Stir together flour and baking soda. Add to butter
mixture; blend well. Stir in macadamia nuts and
chocolate pieces. Drop dough by heaping tablespoons
onto ungreased cookie sheet. Bake 10 to 12 minutes or
until lightly browned. Cool slightly; remove from
cookie sheet to wire rack. Cool completely.

Makes about 2 dozen cookies

Chocolate Chip Caramel Nut Cookies

18 caramels, unwrapped
1 BUTTER FLAVOR* CRISCO® Stick or
   1 cup BUTTER FLAVOR CRISCO
   all-vegetable shortening
1 cup granulated sugar
½ cup firmly packed brown sugar
2 eggs, beaten
2¾ cups all-purpose flour
1 teaspoon baking soda
1 teaspoon salt
1 teaspoon vanilla
½ teaspoon hot water
1 cup semisweet chocolate chips
½ cup coarsely chopped unsalted peanuts

*Butter Flavor Crisco is artificially flavored.

1. Heat oven to 400°F. **Place** sheets of foil on countertop for cooling cookies.

2. Cut each caramel into 4 pieces. **Cut** each piece into 6 pieces.

3. Combine shortening, granulated sugar and brown sugar in large bowl. **Beat** at medium speed of electric mixer until well blended and creamy. **Beat** in eggs.

4. Combine flour, baking soda and salt. **Add** gradually to shortening mixture at low speed of electric mixer. **Mix** until well blended. **Beat** in vanilla and hot water. **Stir** in caramels, chocolate chips and nuts with spoon. **Drop** 2 slightly rounded tablespoonfuls of dough for each cookie, 3 inches apart on ungreased baking sheets. **Shape** dough into circles, 2 inches in diameter and 1 inch high.

5. Bake one baking sheet at a time at 400°F for 7 to 9 minutes or until light golden brown. *Do not overbake.* **Cool** 5 minutes on baking sheets. **Remove** cookies to foil to cool completely.

Makes 2 to 2½ dozen cookies

Island Cookies

1⅔ cups all-purpose flour
¾ teaspoon baking powder
½ teaspoon baking soda
½ teaspoon salt
¾ cup (1½ sticks) butter or margarine, softened
¾ cup packed brown sugar
⅓ cup granulated sugar
1 teaspoon vanilla extract
1 egg
2 cups (11.5-ounce package) NESTLÉ® TOLL HOUSE® Milk Chocolate Morsels
1 cup flaked coconut, toasted if desired
1 cup chopped macadamia nuts or walnuts

COMBINE flour, baking powder, baking soda and salt in small bowl. Beat butter, brown sugar, granulated sugar and vanilla in large mixer bowl until creamy. Beat in egg. Gradually blend in flour mixture. Stir in morsels, coconut and nuts. Drop by slightly rounded tablespoon onto ungreased baking sheets.

BAKE in preheated 375°F. oven for 8 to 11 minutes or until edges are lightly browned. Cool on baking sheets for 2 minutes. Remove to wire racks to cool completely. *Makes about 3 dozen cookies*

Note: NESTLÉ® TOLL HOUSE® Semi-Sweet Chocolate Morsels, Semi-Sweet Chocolate Mini Morsels, Mint-Chocolate Morsels or Premier White Morsels may be substituted for the Milk Chocolate Morsels.

Banana Chocolate Chip Softies

1 **ripe medium banana**
1¼ **cups all-purpose flour**
1 **teaspoon baking powder**
½ **teaspoon salt**
⅓ **cup butter or margarine, softened**
⅓ **cup granulated sugar**
⅓ **cup firmly packed light brown sugar**
1 **large egg**
1 **teaspoon vanilla extract**
1 **cup milk chocolate chips**
½ **cup coarsely chopped walnuts**

1. Preheat oven to 375°F. Lightly grease cookie sheets.

2. Peel banana and place in small bowl. Mash enough banana with fork to measure ½ cup; set aside.

3. Combine flour, baking powder and salt in small bowl. Beat butter, granulated sugar and brown sugar in large bowl with electric mixer at medium speed until light and fluffy, scraping down side of bowl once. Beat in banana, egg and vanilla, scraping down side of bowl once. Add flour mixture. Beat at low speed until well blended, scraping down side of bowl once. Stir in chips and walnuts with mixing spoon. (Dough will be soft.)

4. Drop rounded teaspoonfuls of dough 2 inches apart onto prepared cookie sheets.

5. Bake 9 to 11 minutes until edges are golden brown. Let cookies stand on cookie sheets 2 minutes. Remove cookies to wire racks; cool completely. Store tightly covered at room temperature. (These cookies do not freeze well.) *Makes about 3 dozen cookies*

Peanut Butter Chocolate Chippers

1 **cup creamy or chunky peanut butter**
1 **cup firmly packed light brown sugar**
1 **large egg**
¾ **cup milk chocolate chips**
Granulated sugar

1. Preheat oven to 350°F.

2. Combine peanut butter, sugar and egg in medium bowl; mix with mixing spoon until well blended. Stir in chips.

3. Roll heaping tablespoonfuls of dough into 1½-inch balls. Place balls 2 inches apart on ungreased cookie sheets.

4. Dip table fork into granulated sugar; press criss-cross fashion onto each ball, flattening to ½-inch thickness.

5. Bake 12 minutes or until set. Let cookies stand on cookie sheets 2 minutes. Remove cookies with spatula to wire racks; cool completely. Store tightly covered at room temperature or freeze up to 3 months.

Makes about 2 dozen cookies

Crunchy & Chippy
Peanut Butter Cookies

1¼ cups firmly packed light brown sugar
¾ cup crunchy peanut butter
½ CRISCO® Stick or ½ cup CRISCO
    all-vegetable shortening
3 tablespoons milk
1 tablespoon vanilla
1 egg
1¾ cups all-purpose flour
¾ teaspoon baking soda
¾ teaspoon salt
1 cup (6 ounces) miniature semisweet
    chocolate chips
1 cup chopped peanuts

1. Heat oven to 375°F. **Place** sheets of foil on countertop for cooling cookies. **Place** brown sugar, peanut butter, shortening, milk and vanilla in large bowl. **Beat** at medium speed of electric mixer until well blended. **Add** egg; beat just until blended.

2. Combine flour, baking soda and salt. **Add** to shortening mixture; beat at low speed just until blended. **Stir** in chips and peanuts. **Drop** dough by rounded measuring tablespoonfuls 2 inches apart onto ungreased baking sheets. **Flatten** slightly with fingers.

3. Bake one baking sheet at a time at 375°F for 7 to 8 minutes or until cookies are set and just beginning to brown. *Do not overbake.* **Cool** 2 minutes on baking sheet. **Remove** cookies to foil to cool completely.

Makes about 3 dozen cookies

Peanut Butter Jumbos

½ cup butter or margarine, softened
1 cup packed brown sugar
1 cup granulated sugar
1½ cups peanut butter
3 eggs
2 teaspoons baking soda
1 teaspoon vanilla extract
4½ cups uncooked rolled oats
1 cup (6 ounces) semisweet chocolate chips
1 cup candy-coated chocolate pieces

1. Preheat oven to 350°F. Lightly grease cookie sheets or line with parchment paper.

2. Beat butter, sugars, peanut butter and eggs in large bowl until well blended. Blend in baking soda, vanilla and oats until well mixed. Stir in chips and candy pieces.

3. Scoop out about ⅓ cupful of dough for each cookie. Place on prepared cookie sheets, spacing about 4 inches apart. Press each cookie to flatten slightly. Bake 15 to 20 minutes until firm in center. Remove to wire racks; cool completely. Store tightly covered.

Makes about 1½ dozen cookies

Peanut Butter Chocolate Chip Cookies

    1 **cup sugar**
    ½ **cup SKIPPY® Creamy or SUPER**
           CHUNK® Peanut Butter
    ½ **cup evaporated milk**
    1 **package (6 ounces) semisweet**
           chocolate chips
    1 **cup coarsely chopped nuts**

1. Preheat oven to 325°F. Line large cookie sheets with foil.

2. In medium bowl, stir sugar and peanut butter until smooth. Blend in evaporated milk, chips and nuts. Drop dough by rounded teaspoonfuls 2½ inches apart on prepared foil-lined cookie sheets. Spread batter evenly into 2-inch circles.

3. Bake 18 to 20 minutes or until golden. Cool completely on foil-lined wire racks.

Makes about 3½ dozen cookies

Almond Milk Chocolate Chippers

½ cup slivered almonds
1¼ cups all-purpose flour
½ teaspoon baking soda
½ teaspoon salt
½ cup butter or margarine, softened
½ cup firmly packed light brown sugar
⅓ cup granulated sugar
1 large egg
2 tablespoons almond-flavored liqueur
1 cup milk chocolate chips

1. Preheat oven to 350°F. Spread almonds on baking sheet. Bake 8 to 10 minutes until golden brown, stirring often. Remove almonds from pan; set aside.

2. *Increase oven temperature to 375°F.*

3. Combine flour, baking soda and salt in small bowl. Beat butter, brown sugar and granulated sugar in large bowl with electric mixer at medium speed until light and fluffy, scraping down side of bowl once. Beat in egg until well blended. Beat in liqueur. Gradually add flour mixture. Beat at low speed until well blended. Stir in chips and almonds with mixing spoon.

4. Drop rounded teaspoonfuls of dough 2 inches apart onto ungreased cookie sheets.

5. Bake 9 to 10 minutes until edges are golden brown. Let cookies stand on cookie sheets 2 minutes. Remove cookies with spatula to wire racks; cool completely. Store tightly covered at room temperature or freeze up to 3 months.   *Makes about 3 dozen cookies*

Kids' Favorite Jumbo Chippers

- 1 cup butter or margarine, softened
- ¾ cup granulated sugar
- ¾ cup packed brown sugar
- 2 eggs
- 1 teaspoon vanilla extract
- 2¼ cups all-purpose flour
- 1 teaspoon baking soda
- ¾ teaspoon salt
- 1 (9-ounce) package candy-coated chocolate pieces
- 1 cup peanut butter flavored chips

1. Preheat oven to 375°F.

2. Beat butter, granulated sugar and brown sugar in large bowl until light and fluffy. Beat in eggs and vanilla. Add flour, baking soda and salt. Beat until well blended. Stir in chocolate pieces and peanut butter flavored chips. Drop by rounded tablespoonfuls 3 inches apart onto ungreased cookie sheets.

3. Bake 10 to 12 minutes until edges are golden brown. Let cookies stand on cookie sheets 2 minutes. Remove cookies to wire racks; cool completely. Store tightly covered. *Makes 3 dozen cookies*

Peanut Butter Chip Oatmeal Cookies

 1 cup (2 sticks) butter or margarine,
      softened
 ¼ cup shortening
 2 cups packed light brown sugar
 1 tablespoon milk
 2 teaspoons vanilla extract
 1 egg
 2 cups all-purpose flour
1⅔ cups (10-ounce package) REESE'S®
      Peanut Butter Chips
1½ cups quick-cooking or regular rolled
      oats
 ½ cup chopped walnuts
 ½ teaspoon baking soda
 ½ teaspoon salt

Heat oven to 375°F. In large bowl, beat butter,
shortening, brown sugar, milk, vanilla and egg until
light and fluffy. Add remaining ingredients; mix until
well blended. Drop dough by rounded teaspoons about
2 inches apart onto ungreased cookie sheet. Bake until
light brown, 10 to 12 minutes for soft cookies or 12 to
14 minutes for crisp cookies. Remove from cookie
sheet to wire rack. Cool completely.

Makes 6 dozen cookies

REESE'S® Chewy Chocolate Cookies

    2 cups all-purpose flour
    ¾ cup HERSHEY'S Cocoa
    1 teaspoon baking soda
    ½ teaspoon salt
  1¼ cups (2½ sticks) butter or margarine,
         softened
    2 cups sugar
    2 eggs
    2 teaspoons vanilla extract
  1⅔ cups (10-ounce package) REESE'S®
         Peanut Butter Chips

Heat oven to 350°F. Stir together flour, cocoa, baking
soda and salt. In large bowl, beat butter and sugar with
electric mixer until light and fluffy. Add eggs and
vanilla; beat well. Gradually add flour mixture, beating
well. Stir in peanut butter chips. Drop by rounded
teaspoons onto ungreased cookie sheet. Bake 8 to 9
minutes. *(Do not overbake; cookies will be soft. They
will puff while baking and flatten while cooling.)* Cool
slightly; remove from cookie sheet to wire rack. Cool
completely.   *Makes about 4½ dozen cookies*

Pan Recipe: Spread batter in greased 15½×10½×1-inch
jelly-roll pan. Bake at 350°F, 20 minutes or until set.
Cool completely in pan on wire rack; cut into bars.
Makes about 4 dozen bars.

Ice Cream Sandwiches: Prepare REESE'S® Chewy
Chocolate Cookies as directed; cool. Press small scoop
of vanilla ice cream between flat sides of cookies. Wrap
and freeze.

Double Chocolate Chip Cookies

    2 cups all-purpose flour
    1 teaspoon baking soda
    ½ teaspoon salt
    4 cups (24-ounce package) HERSHEY'S
        Semi-Sweet Chocolate Chips, divided
    ¾ cup (1½ sticks) butter or margarine,
        softened
    ¾ cup sugar
    2 eggs

Heat oven to 350°F. Stir together flour, baking soda and salt. In medium microwave-safe bowl, place 2 cups chocolate chips. Microwave at HIGH (100%) 1½ minutes; stir. Microwave at HIGH an additional 15 seconds at a time stirring after each heating or until chips are melted and smooth when stirred; cool slightly.

In large bowl, beat butter and sugar until light and fluffy. Add eggs; beat well. Stir in melted chocolate. Gradually add flour mixture to chocolate mixture, beating well. Stir in remaining 2 cups chips. Drop dough by rounded teaspoons onto ungreased cookie sheet. Bake 8 to 9 minutes. *Do not overbake.* Cookies should be soft. Cool slightly. Remove from cookie sheet to wire rack; cool completely.

Makes about 5 dozen cookies

Deep Dark Chocolate Cookies

¾ cup (1½ sticks) butter or margarine,
    softened
¾ cup granulated sugar
½ cup packed light brown sugar
1 teaspoon vanilla extract
2 eggs
1¾ cups all-purpose flour
½ cup HERSHEY'S Cocoa or HERSHEY'S
    European Style Cocoa
¾ teaspoon baking soda
½ teaspoon baking powder
¼ teaspoon salt
1 cup HERSHEY'S Semi-Sweet
    Chocolate Chips
½ cup chopped nuts

Heat oven to 375°F. In large bowl, beat butter,
granulated sugar, brown sugar and vanilla on medium
speed of electric mixer until creamy. Add eggs; beat
well. Stir together flour, cocoa, baking soda, baking
powder and salt; gradually add to butter mixture,
beating just until blended. Stir in chocolate chips and
nuts. Drop by heaping teaspoonfuls onto ungreased
cookie sheet. Bake 7 minutes or until set. Cool
1 minute; remove from cookie sheet to wire rack. Cool
completely.   *Makes about 4 dozen cookies*

Chocolatetown Chip Cookies

¾ cup (1½ sticks) butter (do *not* use
    margarine), softened
1 cup packed light brown sugar
½ cup granulated sugar
1 teaspoon vanilla extract
2 eggs
2 cups all-purpose flour
1 teaspoon baking soda
1 teaspoon salt
2 cups (12-ounce package) HERSHEY'S
    Semi-Sweet Chocolate Chips

Heat oven to 375°F. In large bowl, beat butter, brown
sugar, granulated sugar and vanilla until creamy. Add
eggs; beat well. Stir together flour, baking soda and
salt; gradually add to butter mixture, beating until
blended. Stir in chocolate chips. Drop dough by
teaspoons onto ungreased cookie sheet. Bake 8 to
10 minutes or until lightly browned. Remove from
cookie sheet to wire rack. Cool completely.

Makes about 7 dozen cookies

Almond Double Chip Cookies

¾ cup butter or margarine, softened
¾ cup packed light brown sugar
1 egg
½ teaspoon almond extract
1½ cups all-purpose flour
¼ teaspoon baking soda
Dash salt
1 cup (6 ounces) semisweet chocolate
   chips
1 cup (6 ounces) vanilla milk chips
½ cup slivered blanched almonds

1. Preheat oven to 375°F. Line cookie sheets with parchment paper or leave ungreased.

2. Beat butter and brown sugar in large bowl with electric mixer until creamy. Beat in egg and almond extract.

3. Combine flour, baking soda and salt in small bowl; blend into butter mixture. Stir in semisweet chocolate chips, vanilla milk chips and almonds. Drop by rounded tablespoonfuls, 3 inches apart, onto prepared cookie sheets.

4. Bake 8 to 10 minutes until lightly browned. *Do not overbake.* Cool 2 minutes on cookie sheets; remove to wire racks. Cool completely. Store tightly covered.

Makes about 3 dozen cookies

Brownie Cookie Bites

1½ cups (9 ounces) NESTLÉ® TOLL
      HOUSE® Semi-Sweet Chocolate
      Morsels, *divided*
  1 tablespoon butter
  ¼ cup all-purpose flour
  ¼ teaspoon baking powder
  1 egg
  ⅓ cup granulated sugar
  ½ teaspoon vanilla extract

MELT *½ cup* morsels and butter over hot (not boiling) water, stirring until smooth. Combine flour and baking powder in small bowl; set aside.

BEAT egg and sugar in large mixer bowl at high speed for about 3 minutes or until mixture is thickened. Stir in vanilla and melted chocolate mixture. Gradually blend in flour mixture. Stir in *remaining* 1 cup morsels. Drop by level tablespoon onto greased baking sheets.

BAKE in preheated 350°F. oven for 8 to 10 minutes or until cookies are puffed and tops are cracked and moist (cookies will appear slightly underbaked). Cool on baking sheets for 5 minutes. Remove to wire racks to cool completely. *Makes about 1½ dozen cookies*

Double Nut Chocolate Chip Cookies

1 package DUNCAN HINES® Moist
  Deluxe Yellow Cake Mix
½ cup butter or margarine, melted
1 egg
1 cup semi-sweet chocolate chips
½ cup finely chopped pecans
1 cup sliced almonds, divided

1. Preheat oven to 375°F. Grease baking sheets.

2. Combine cake mix, butter and egg in large bowl. Mix at low speed with electric mixer until just blended. Stir in chocolate chips, pecans and ¼ cup of the almonds. Shape rounded tablespoonfuls of dough into balls. Place remaining ¾ cup almonds in shallow bowl. Press tops of cookies in almonds. Place 1 inch apart on prepared baking sheets.

3. Bake at 375°F for 9 to 11 minutes or until lightly browned. Cool 2 minutes on baking sheets. Remove to cooling racks. Cool completely. Store in airtight containers.   *Makes 3 to 3½ dozen cookies*

Original NESTLÉ® TOLL HOUSE® Chocolate Chip Cookies

2¼ cups all-purpose flour
1 teaspoon baking soda
1 teaspoon salt
1 cup (2 sticks) butter, softened
¾ cup granulated sugar
¾ cup packed brown sugar
1 teaspoon vanilla extract
2 eggs
2 cups (12-ounce package) NESTLÉ®
     TOLL HOUSE® Semi-Sweet
     Chocolate Morsels
1 cup chopped nuts

COMBINE flour, baking soda and salt in small bowl. Beat butter, granulated sugar, brown sugar and vanilla in large mixer bowl. Add eggs one at a time, beating well after each addition; gradually beat in flour mixture. Stir in morsels and nuts. Drop by rounded tablespoon onto ungreased baking sheets.

BAKE in preheated 375°F. oven for 9 to 11 minutes or until golden brown. Cool on baking sheets for 2 minutes; remove to wire racks to cool completely.

Makes about 5 dozen cookies

Pan Cookie Variation: Prepare dough as above. Spread into greased 15½×10½-inch jelly-roll pan. Bake in preheated 375°F. oven for 20 to 25 minutes or until golden brown. Cool in pan on wire rack. Makes 4 dozen bars.

Crunchy Chocolate Chipsters

1¼ cups packed light brown sugar
¾ **BUTTER FLAVOR* CRISCO®** Stick or
    ¾ cup **BUTTER FLAVOR CRISCO**
    all-vegetable shortening
2 tablespoons milk
1 tablespoon vanilla
1 egg
1½ cups flour
1 teaspoon salt
¾ teaspoon baking soda
2 cups crispy rice cereal
1 cup semisweet miniature chocolate
    chips

1. Heat oven to 375°F. **Place** sheets of foil on countertop for cooling cookies.

2. Combine brown sugar, shortening, milk and vanilla in large bowl. **Beat** at medium speed of electric mixer until well blended. **Beat** egg into shortening mixture.

3. Combine flour, salt and baking soda. **Mix** into shortening mixture just until blended. **Stir** in cereal and chocolate chips.

4. Drop by rounded tablespoonfuls 2 inches apart onto ungreased baking sheets.

5. Bake one baking sheet at a time at 375°F for 10 to 12 minutes. *Do not overbake.* **Cool** 2 minutes on baking sheets. **Remove** cookies to foil to cool completely.   *Makes about 3 dozen cookies*

*Butter Flavor Crisco is artificially flavored.

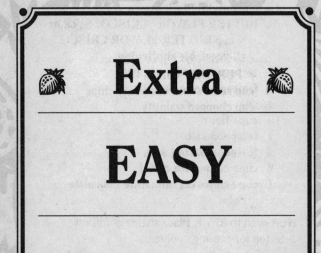

Extra

EASY

Devil's Food Fudge Cookies

1 package DUNCAN HINES® Moist
    Deluxe Devil's Food Cake Mix
2 eggs
½ cup CRISCO® Oil or CRISCO®
    PURITAN® Canola Oil
1 cup semi-sweet chocolate chips
½ cup chopped walnuts

1. Preheat oven to 350°F. Grease baking sheets.

2. Combine cake mix, eggs and oil in large bowl. Stir until thoroughly blended. Stir in chocolate chips and walnuts. (Mixture will be stiff.) Shape dough into 36 (1¼-inch) balls. Place 2 inches apart on greased baking sheets. Bake at 350°F for 10 to 11 minutes. (Cookies will look moist.) *Do not overbake.* Cool 2 minutes on baking sheets. Remove to cooling racks. Cool completely. Store in airtight container.

Makes 3 dozen cookies

Chocolate Candy Cookies

⅔ cup MIRACLE WHIP® Salad Dressing
1 two-layer devil's food cake mix
2 eggs
1 (8-ounce) package candy-coated
    chocolate candies

PREHEAT oven to 375°F.

BLEND salad dressing, cake mix and eggs at low speed with electric mixer until moistened. Beat on medium speed 2 minutes. Stir in chocolate candies. (Dough will be stiff.)

DROP by rounded teaspoonfuls, 2 inches apart, onto greased cookie sheets.

BAKE 9 to 11 minutes or until almost set. (Cookies will still appear soft.) Cool 1 minute; remove from cookie sheets.   *Makes about 4½ dozen cookies*

Quick Chocolate Softies

1 package (18.25 ounces) devil's food
    cake mix
⅓ cup water
¼ cup butter or margarine, softened
1 egg
1 cup white chocolate baking chips
½ cup coarsely chopped walnuts

1. Preheat oven to 350°F. Grease cookie sheets.

2. Combine cake mix, water, butter and egg in large bowl. Beat with electric mixer at low speed until moistened, scraping down side of bowl once. Increase speed to medium; beat 1 minute, scraping down side of bowl once. (Dough will be thick.) Stir in chips and nuts; mix until well blended. Drop dough by heaping teaspoonfuls 2 inches apart onto prepared cookie sheets.

3. Bake 10 to 12 minutes until set. Let cookies stand on cookie sheets 1 minute. Remove cookies to wire racks; cool completely. Store tightly covered.

Makes about 4 dozen cookies

OREO® Brownie Treats

15 **OREO® Chocolate Sandwich Cookies,**
   coarsely chopped
 1 **(21½-ounce) package deluxe fudge**
   brownie mix, batter prepared
   according to package directions
 2 **pints ice cream, any flavor**

Stir cookie pieces into prepared brownie batter. Grease 13×9-inch baking pan; pour batter into pan. Bake according to brownie mix package directions for time and temperature. Cool. To serve, cut into 12 squares and top each with a scoop of ice cream.

Makes 12 servings

Quick & Easy Fudgey Brownies

4   bars (1 ounce each) HERSHEY'S
      Unsweetened Baking Chocolate,
      broken into pieces
¾   cup (1½ sticks) butter or margarine
2   cups sugar
3   eggs
1½   teaspoons vanilla extract
1   cup all-purpose flour
1   cup chopped nuts (optional)
      Creamy Quick Chocolate Frosting
      (recipe follows, optional)

Heat oven to 350°F. Grease 13×9×2-inch baking pan.
In large microwave-safe bowl, place chocolate and
butter. Microwave at HIGH (100%) 1½ to 2 minutes or
until chocolate is melted and mixture is smooth when
stirred. Add sugar; stir with spoon until well blended.
Add eggs and vanilla; mix well. Add flour and nuts, if
desired; stir until well blended. Spread into prepared
pan. Bake 30 to 35 minutes or until wooden pick
inserted in center comes out almost clean. Cool
completely in pan on wire rack. Frost with Creamy
Quick Chocolate Frosting, if desired. Cut into squares.
Makes about 24 brownies

Creamy Quick Chocolate Frosting

3 tablespoons butter or margarine
3 bars (1 ounce each) HERSHEY‚S
   Unsweetened Baking Chocolate,
   broken into pieces
3 cups powdered sugar
½ cup milk
1 teaspoon vanilla extract
⅛ teaspoon salt

In small saucepan over very low heat, melt butter; add chocolate pieces. Cook, stirring constantly, until chocolate is melted and mixture is smooth. Pour into large bowl. Add powdered sugar, milk, vanilla and salt; beat on medium speed of electric mixer until well blended. Refrigerate 10 to 15 minutes or until of spreading consistency.

Makes about 2 cups frosting

Special Treat No-Bake Squares

½ cup plus 1 teaspoon butter or
    margarine, divided
¼ cup granulated sugar
¼ cup unsweetened cocoa powder
1 egg
¼ teaspoon salt
1½ cups graham cracker crumbs
¾ cup flaked coconut
½ cup chopped pecans
⅓ cup butter or margarine, softened
1 package (3 ounces) cream cheese,
    softened
1 teaspoon vanilla extract
1 cup powdered sugar
1 (2-ounce) semisweet or bittersweet
    candy bar, broken into ½-inch pieces

1. Line 9-inch square pan with foil, shiny side up, allowing a 2-inch overhang on sides.

2. For crust, combine ½ cup butter, granulated sugar, cocoa, egg and salt in medium saucepan. Cook over medium heat, stirring constantly, until mixture thickens, about 2 minutes. Remove from heat; stir in graham cracker crumbs, coconut and pecans. Press evenly into prepared baking pan.

3. For filling, beat ⅓ cup softened butter, cream cheese and vanilla in medium bowl until smooth. Gradually beat in powdered sugar. Spread over crust; refrigerate 30 minutes.

4. For glaze, combine candy bar and remaining 1 teaspoon butter in small resealable plastic bag; seal. Microwave at HIGH 50 seconds. Turn bag over; heat at HIGH 40 to 50 seconds until melted. Knead bag until candy bar is smooth. Cut pinpoint hole in corner of bag; drizzle chocolate over filling. Refrigerate until firm, about 20 minutes. Remove foil from pan. Cut into 1½-inch squares. Store tightly covered.

Makes about 25 squares

No-Fuss Bar Cookies

2 cups graham cracker crumbs (about 24 graham cracker squares)
1 cup semisweet chocolate chips
1 cup flaked coconut
¾ cup coarsely chopped walnuts
1 can (14 ounces) sweetened condensed milk

1. Preheat oven to 350°F. Grease 13×9-inch baking pan.

2. Combine crumbs, chocolate chips, coconut and walnuts in large bowl; stir to blend. Add milk; mix until blended. Spread batter in prepared pan.

3. Bake 15 to 18 minutes until edges are golden brown. Let pan stand on wire rack until completely cooled. Cut into 2¼-inch squares. Store tightly covered.

Makes about 20 cookies

Chocolate Chip Macaroons

2½ cups flaked coconut
⅔ cup mini semisweet chocolate chips
⅔ cup sweetened condensed milk
1 teaspoon vanilla extract

1. Preheat oven to 350°F. Grease cookie sheets.

2. Combine coconut, chocolate chips, milk and vanilla in medium bowl; mix until well blended. Drop dough by rounded teaspoonfuls 2 inches apart onto prepared cookie sheets. Press dough gently with back of spoon to flatten slightly.

3. Bake 10 to 12 minutes until light golden brown. Let cookies stand on cookie sheets 1 minute. Remove cookies to wire racks; cool completely. Store tightly covered.   *Makes about 3½ dozen cookies*

Easy Party Cookies Made with "M & M's"® Chocolate Candies

2¼ cups all-purpose flour
1 teaspoon salt
1 teaspoon baking soda
1 cup butter or margarine, softened
1 cup packed light brown sugar
½ cup granulated sugar
2 eggs
2 teaspoons vanilla
1½ cups "M & M's"® Plain Chocolate
    Candies, divided

Preheat oven to 375°F. In medium bowl, combine flour, salt and baking soda. Set aside.

In large bowl, beat butter, brown sugar and granulated sugar until light and fluffy. Blend in eggs and vanilla. Gradually beat in flour mixture; mix well. Stir in ½ cup candies. Drop by rounded teaspoonfuls onto ungreased cookie sheets. Press 2 or 3 additional candies into each cookie.

Bake 10 to 12 minutes or until golden brown. Cool completely on wire racks.

Makes about 6 dozen cookies

NESTLÉ® CRUNCH® Pizza Cookie

- 1 **cup plus 2 tablespoons all-purpose flour**
- ¼ **teaspoon baking soda**
- ¼ **teaspoon salt**
- ½ **cup (1 stick) butter or margarine, softened**
- 6 **tablespoons granulated sugar**
- 6 **tablespoons packed brown sugar**
- 1 **egg**
- ½ **teaspoon vanilla extract**
- 1¾ **cups (8-ounce package) NESTLÉ® CRUNCH® Baking Pieces, *divided***
- ½ **cup peanut butter**

COMBINE flour, baking soda and salt in small bowl. Beat butter, granulated sugar and brown sugar in large mixer bowl. Beat in egg and vanilla. Gradually beat in flour mixture. Stir in *½ cup* CRUNCH® Baking Pieces. Spread or pat dough onto bottom of greased 13×9-inch baking pan or 12-inch pizza pan.

BAKE in preheated 350°F. oven for 14 to 18 minutes or until set and deep golden brown. Remove from oven. Drop peanut butter by spoonfuls onto hot crust; let stand for 5 minutes to soften. Gently spread over crust. Sprinkle *remaining* CRUNCH® Baking Pieces in single layer over peanut butter. Serve warm or at room temperature. *Makes about 12 servings*

Pecan Caramel Bars

1½ cups all-purpose flour
1½ cups packed brown sugar, divided
½ cup butter, softened
1 cup pecan halves
⅔ cup butter
1 cup milk chocolate pieces

Preheat oven to 350°F. In large mixer bowl, combine flour, 1 cup brown sugar and ½ cup butter. Beat 2 to 3 minutes or until mixture resembles fine crumbs. Pat mixture evenly onto bottom of ungreased 13×9-inch baking pan. Sprinkle nuts evenly over crumb mixture.

In small saucepan, combine ⅔ cup butter and remaining ½ cup brown sugar. Cook and stir over medium heat until entire surface is bubbly. Cook and stir up to 1 minute more. Pour over crust, spreading evenly.

Bake 18 to 20 minutes or until entire surface is bubbly. Remove from oven; immediately sprinkle with chocolate pieces. Let stand 2 to 3 minutes to allow chocolate to melt; use knife to swirl chocolate slightly. Cool completely on wire rack. Cut into bars.

Makes 4 dozen bars

Favorite recipe from **Wisconsin Milk Marketing Board**

Chocolate Butterscotch Drops

½ cup semi-sweet chocolate chips
1 cup butterscotch chips
1 cup dry roasted peanuts
2 cups KELLOGG'S® CRISPIX® cereal

1. In heavy 2-quart saucepan melt chips over low heat, stirring constantly. Remove from heat. Stir in peanuts and KELLOGG'S® CRISPIX® cereal.

2. Drop by measuring tablespoons onto waxed paper. Refrigerate until firm. Store in airtight container in refrigerator.   *Makes 2 dozen drops*

Microwave Directions: In large microwave-safe mixing bowl, melt chocolate and butterscotch chips on HIGH (100% power) 1 minute. Stir chips and heat on HIGH (100% power) an additional 30 seconds until melted. Stir in peanuts and cereal. Follow step 2 above.

No-Bake Cherry Crisps

¼ cup butter or margarine, softened
1 cup powdered sugar
1 cup peanut butter
¼ cup plus 2 tablespoons mini semisweet
    chocolate chips
¼ cup chopped pecans
1⅓ cups crisp rice cereal
½ cup maraschino cherries, drained, dried
    and chopped
1 to 2 cups flaked coconut for rolling

1. Beat butter, sugar and peanut butter in large bowl with electric mixer at medium speed until creamy. Stir in chips, pecans, cereal and cherries; mix well.

2. Shape teaspoonfuls of dough into 1-inch balls. Roll in coconut. Place on cookie sheets and chill in refrigerator 1 hour. Store in refrigerator.

Makes about 3 dozen cookies

Crispy Chocolate Bars

> 1 **package (6 ounces, 1 cup) semi-sweet chocolate chips**
> 1 **package (6 ounces, 1 cup) butterscotch chips**
> ½ **cup peanut butter**
> 5 **cups KELLOGG'S CORN FLAKES® cereal**
>   **Vegetable cooking spray**

1. In large saucepan, combine chocolate and butterscotch chips and peanut butter. Stir over low heat until smooth. Remove from heat.

2. Add KELLOGG'S CORN FLAKES® cereal. Stir until well coated.

3. Using buttered spatula or waxed paper, press mixture evenly into 9×9×2-inch pan coated with cooking spray. Cut into bars when cool. *Makes 16 bars*

Easy Linzer Bars

- 2 cups flour
- ½ cup sugar
- ¾ teaspoon baking soda
- ½ teaspoon cinnamon
- ½ teaspoon grated lemon peel
- ½ cup (1 stick) MAZOLA® Margarine or butter
- ¼ cup KARO® Light Corn Syrup
- ½ cup seedless raspberry preserves
- ⅓ cup finely chopped walnuts
- ⅔ cup confectioners sugar
- 1 tablespoon milk

1. Preheat oven to 350°F. In large bowl combine flour, sugar, baking soda, cinnamon and lemon peel; set aside.

2. In small saucepan heat margarine and corn syrup over low heat until margarine melts. Stir into flour mixture until blended. Divide dough into 5 equal pieces.

3. On large ungreased cookie sheet, pat each piece of dough into 14×1-inch rope. Combine raspberry preserves and walnuts. Make an indentation down center of each rope; fill with preserve mixture, mounding slightly.

4. Bake 12 to 14 minutes or until lightly browned. Remove from oven; immediately cut diagonally into 1-inch-wide slices.

5. In small bowl stir confectioners sugar and milk until smooth. Drizzle over warm cookies. Cool on wire racks. Store in airtight container.

Makes about 5 dozen cookies

Lemon Cookies

1   package DUNCAN HINES® Moist
      Deluxe Lemon Supreme Cake Mix
2   eggs
⅓   cup CRISCO® Oil or CRISCO®
      PURITAN® Canola Oil
1   tablespoon lemon juice
¾   cup chopped nuts or flaked coconut
      Confectioners sugar

1. Preheat oven to 375°F. Grease baking sheets.

2. Combine cake mix, eggs, oil and lemon juice in large bowl. Beat at low speed with electric mixer until well blended. Add nuts. Shape into 1-inch balls. Place 1 inch apart on greased baking sheets. Bake at 375°F for 6 to 7 minutes or until lightly browned. Cool 1 minute on baking sheets. Remove to cooling racks. Sprinkle with confectioners sugar. Cool completely. Store in airtight containers.   *Makes about 3 dozen cookies*

Tip: You can frost cookies with 1 cup confectioners sugar mixed with 1 tablespoon lemon juice instead of sprinkling cookies with confectioners sugar.

Orange Pecan Gems

1 **package DUNCAN HINES® Moist
   Deluxe Orange Supreme Cake Mix**
1 **container (8 ounces) vanilla low fat
   yogurt**
1 **egg**
2 **tablespoons butter or margarine,
   softened**
1 **cup finely chopped pecans**
1 **cup pecan halves**

1. Preheat oven to 350°F. Grease baking sheets.

2. Combine cake mix, yogurt, egg, butter and chopped
pecans in large bowl. Beat at low speed with electric
mixer until blended. Drop by rounded teaspoonfuls
2 inches apart onto greased baking sheets. Press pecan
half onto center of each cookie. Bake at 350°F for 11 to
13 minutes or until golden brown. Cool 1 minute on
baking sheets. Remove to cooling racks. Cool
completely. Store in airtight container.

Makes about 4½ to 5 dozen cookies

Date-Oatmeal Cookies

1   **cup all-purpose flour**
¾   **cup quick-cooking oats**
1   **cup DOLE® Pitted Dates or Pitted**
      Prunes, chopped
1   **teaspoon ground cinnamon**
¾   **teaspoon baking powder**
¼   **cup light margarine, softened**
⅔   **cup packed brown sugar**
1   **egg**
1   **medium, ripe DOLE® Banana, mashed**
      (about ½ cup)
1   **teaspoon vanilla extract**
      Vegetable cooking spray

• **Combine** flour, oats, dates, cinnamon and baking powder in medium bowl; set aside.

• **Beat** margarine and sugar in large bowl until well blended. Add egg, banana and vanilla; beat until blended. Stir in flour mixture until just moistened.

• **Drop** dough by rounded teaspoonfuls, 2 inches apart, onto baking sheets sprayed with vegetable cooking spray.

• **Bake** at 375°F 10 to 12 minutes or until cookies are firm and bottoms are browned. Remove cookies to wire rack; cool. Store in airtight container.

Makes 32 cookies

Spicy Oatmeal Raisin Cookies

1   package DUNCAN HINES® Moist
      Deluxe Spice Cake Mix
4   egg whites
1   cup quick-cooking oats (not instant or
      old-fashioned), uncooked
½   cup CRISCO® Oil or CRISCO®
      PURITAN® Canola Oil
½   cup raisins

1. Preheat oven to 350°F. Grease baking sheets.

2. Combine cake mix, egg whites, oats and oil in large mixer bowl. Beat on low speed with electric mixer until blended. Stir in raisins. Drop by rounded teaspoons onto greased baking sheets. Bake at 350°F for 7 to 9 minutes or until lightly browned. Cool 1 minute on baking sheets. Remove to cooling racks. Cool completely. Store in airtight container.

Makes about 4 dozen cookies

Chocolate Chip 'n' Oatmeal Cookies

1 package (18.25 or 18.5 ounces) yellow
   cake mix
1 cup rolled oats, uncooked
¾ cup butter or margarine, softened
2 eggs
1 cup HERSHEY'S Semi-Sweet
   Chocolate Chips

Heat oven to 350°F. In large bowl, combine cake mix,
oats, butter and eggs; mix well. Stir in chocolate chips.
Drop by rounded teaspoons onto ungreased cookie
sheet. Bake 10 to 12 minutes or until very lightly
browned. Cool slightly; remove from cookie sheet to
wire rack. Cool completely.

Makes about 4 dozen cookies

Quick Peanut Butter Chocolate Chip Cookies

1   package DUNCAN HINES® Moist
      Deluxe Yellow Cake Mix
½   cup JIF® Creamy Peanut Butter
½   cup butter or margarine, softened
2   eggs
1   cup milk chocolate chips

1. Preheat oven to 350°F. Grease baking sheets.

2. Combine cake mix, peanut butter, butter and eggs in large bowl. Mix at low speed with electric mixer until blended. Stir in chocolate chips. Drop by rounded teaspoonfuls onto greased baking sheets. Bake at 350°F for 9 to 11 minutes or until lightly browned. Cool 2 minutes on baking sheets. Remove to cooling racks. Cool completely. Store in airtight container.

Makes about 4 dozen cookies

Chocolate Peanut Butter Cookies

1   package DUNCAN HINES® Moist
      Deluxe Devil's Food Cake Mix
¾   cup JIF® Extra Crunchy Peanut Butter
2   eggs
2   tablespoons milk
1   cup candy-coated peanut butter pieces

1. Preheat oven to 350°F. Grease baking sheets.

2. Combine cake mix, peanut butter, eggs and milk in large bowl. Mix at low speed with electric mixer until blended. Stir in peanut butter pieces. Drop dough by slightly rounded tablespoonfuls onto prepared baking sheets. Bake at 350°F for 7 to 9 minutes or until lightly browned. Cool 2 minutes on baking sheets. Remove to cooling racks. Cool completely. Store in airtight container. *Makes about 3½ dozen cookies*

P. B. Graham Snackers

- ½ **BUTTER FLAVOR* CRISCO® Stick** or ½ cup **BUTTER FLAVOR CRISCO** all-vegetable shortening
- 2 cups powdered sugar
- ¾ cup creamy peanut butter
- 1 cup graham cracker crumbs
- ½ cup semisweet chocolate chips
- ½ cup graham cracker crumbs or crushed peanuts or chocolate sprinkles (optional)

1. Combine shortening, powdered sugar and peanut butter in large bowl. **Beat** at low speed of electric mixer until well blended. **Stir** in 1 cup crumbs and chocolate chips. **Cover** and refrigerate 1 hour.

2. Form dough into 1-inch balls. **Roll** in ½ cup crumbs. **Cover** and refrigerate until ready to serve.

Makes about 3 dozen cookies

*Butter Flavor Crisco is artificially flavored.

No-Bake Peanutty Cookies

2 cups Roasted Honey Nut SKIPPY®
    Creamy or SUPER CHUNK® Peanut
    Butter
2 cups graham cracker crumbs
1 cup confectioners sugar
½ cup KARO® Light or Dark Corn Syrup
¼ cup semisweet chocolate chips, melted
    Colored sprinkles (optional)

1. In large bowl combine peanut butter, graham cracker crumbs, confectioners sugar and corn syrup. Mix until smooth. Shape into 1-inch balls. Place on waxed paper-lined cookie sheets.

2. Drizzle melted chocolate over balls; roll in colored sprinkles if desired. Store covered in refrigerator.

Makes about 5 dozen cookies

Easy Peanutty Snickerdoodles

2 tablespoons sugar
2 teaspoons ground cinnamon
1 package (22.3 ounces) golden sugar
   cookie mix
2 eggs
⅓ cup vegetable oil
1 tablespoon water
1 cup REESE'S® Peanut Butter Chips

Heat oven to 375°F. Stir together sugar and cinnamon;
set aside. Empty cookie mix into large bowl. Break up
any lumps. Add egg, oil and water; stir with spoon or
fork until well blended. Stir in peanut butter chips.
Shape dough into 1-inch balls. (If dough is too soft to
handle, cover and refrigerate about 1 hour.) Roll balls
in cinnamon-sugar; place on ungreased cookie sheet.
Bake 9 to 11 minutes or until set. Cool slightly; remove
from cookie sheet to wire rack. Cool completely.

Makes about 3½ dozen cookies

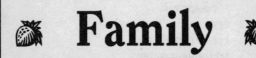

Family

FAVORITES

Peanut Blossoms

1 bag (9 ounces) HERSHEY¿S KISSES₀
   Milk Chocolates
½ cup shortening
¾ cup REESE'S₀ Creamy or Crunchy
   Peanut Butter
⅓ cup granulated sugar
⅓ cup packed light brown sugar
1 egg
2 tablespoons milk
1 teaspoon vanilla extract
1½ cups all-purpose flour
1 teaspoon baking soda
½ teaspoon salt
   Granulated sugar

Heat oven to 375°F. Remove wrappers from chocolate
pieces. In large bowl, beat shortening and peanut
butter with electric mixer until well blended. Add
⅓ cup granulated sugar and brown sugar; beat until
light and fluffy. Add egg, milk and vanilla; beat well.
Stir together flour, baking soda and salt; gradually add
to peanut butter mixture. Shape dough into 1-inch
balls. Roll in granulated sugar; place on ungreased
cookie sheet. Bake 10 to 12 minutes or until lightly
browned. Immediately place chocolate piece on top of
each cookie, pressing down so cookie cracks around
edges. Remove from cookie sheet to wire rack. Cool
completely.   *Makes about 4 dozen cookies*

Peanut Butter Sombreros

1¼ cups firmly packed light brown sugar
¾ cup creamy peanut butter
½ CRISCO® Stick or ½ cup CRISCO all-vegetable shortening
3 tablespoons milk
1 tablespoon vanilla
1 egg
1¾ cups all-purpose flour
¾ teaspoon baking soda
¾ teaspoon salt
Granulated sugar
40 to 50 chocolate kisses, unwrapped

1. Heat oven to 375°F. **Place** sheets of foil on countertop for cooling cookies.

2. Place brown sugar, peanut butter, shortening, milk and vanilla in large bowl. **Beat** at medium speed of electric mixer until well blended. **Add** egg; beat just until blended.

3. Combine flour, baking soda and salt. **Add** to shortening mixture; beat at low speed just until blended.

4. Shape dough into 1-inch balls. **Roll** in granulated sugar. **Place** 2 inches apart on ungreased baking sheets.

5. Bake one baking sheet at a time at 375°F for 6 minutes. **Press** chocolate kiss into center of each cookie. **Bake** 3 minutes longer. *Do not overbake.* **Cool** 2 minutes on baking sheet. **Remove** cookies to foil to cool completely. *Makes about 4 dozen cookies*

Peanut Butter Treats

1¼ cups firmly packed light brown sugar
¾ BUTTER FLAVOR* CRISCO® Stick or
¾ cup BUTTER FLAVOR CRISCO
all-vegetable shortening
2 tablespoons milk
1 tablespoon vanilla
1 egg
1¾ cups all-purpose flour
1 teaspoon salt
¾ teaspoon baking soda
2 cups (about 32) miniature peanut
butter cups, unwrapped and
quartered or coarsely chopped

1. Heat oven to 375°F. **Place** sheets of foil on
countertop for cooling cookies.

2. Place brown sugar, shortening, milk and vanilla in
large bowl. **Beat** at medium speed of electric mixer
until well blended. **Add** egg; beat well.

3. Combine flour, salt and baking soda. **Add** to
shortening mixture; beat at low speed just until
blended. **Stir** in peanut butter cup quarters.

4. Drop dough by rounded measuring tablespoonfuls
3 inches apart onto ungreased baking sheets.

5. Bake one baking sheet at a time at 375°F for 8 to
10 minutes or until cookies are lightly browned. *Do
not overbake.* **Cool** 2 minutes on baking sheet. **Remove**
cookies to foil to cool completely.

Makes about 3 dozen cookies

*Butter Flavor Crisco is artificially flavored.

Inside-Out Peanut Butter Cookie Cups

COOKIES
- 1¼ cups firmly packed light brown sugar
- ¾ cup creamy peanut butter
- ½ CRISCO® Stick or ½ cup CRISCO all-vegetable shortening
- 3 tablespoons milk
- 1 tablespoon vanilla
- 1 egg
- 1¾ cups all-purpose flour
- ¾ teaspoon baking soda
- ¾ teaspoon salt

FILLING
- 1 cup (6 ounces) semi-sweet chocolate chips
- 1 teaspoon BUTTER FLAVOR* CRISCO all-vegetable shortening**
- ¼ cup finely chopped peanuts

*Butter Flavor Crisco is artificially flavored.

**Crisco all-vegetable shortening can be substituted for Butter Flavor Crisco.

1. *For cookies,* **place** brown sugar, peanut butter, shortening, milk and vanilla in large bowl. **Beat** at medium speed of electric mixer until well blended. **Add** egg; beat just until blended.

2. Combine flour, baking soda and salt. **Add** to shortening mixture; beat at low speed just until blended. **Refrigerate** about 1 hour or until firm.

3. Heat oven to 375°F. **Grease** mini-muffin pans (1¾ inches in diameter). **Place** sheets of foil on countertop for cooling cookies.

4. Shape dough into 1-inch balls. **Place** each ball in prepared mini-muffin cup. **Press** dough onto bottom and sides of cup to within ½ inch of top.

5. Bake at 375°F for 7 to 8 minutes or until cookies are set and just beginning to brown. *Do not overbake.* **Cool** 10 minutes on cooling racks. **Remove** cookie cups carefully to foil to cool completely.

6. *For filling,* place chocolate chips and shortening in medium microwave-safe bowl. **Microwave** at 50% (MEDIUM) for 1 to 2 minutes or until chips are shiny and soft. **Stir** until smooth. **Spoon** about ½ teaspoon chocolate mixture into center of each cookie. **Sprinkle** with chopped peanuts. **Cool** completely.

Makes about 3½ dozen cookie cups

Double-Dipped Chocolate Peanut Butter Cookies

1¼ cups all-purpose flour
½ teaspoon baking powder
½ teaspoon baking soda
½ teaspoon salt
½ cup butter or margarine, softened
½ cup granulated sugar
½ cup packed light brown sugar
⅓ cup creamy or chunky peanut butter
1 large egg
1 teaspoon vanilla extract
   Additional granulated sugar
1½ cups semisweet chocolate chips
1½ cups milk chocolate chips
3 teaspoons shortening, divided

1. Preheat oven to 350°F.

2. Combine flour, baking powder, baking soda and salt in small bowl. Beat butter, ½ cup granulated sugar and brown sugar in large bowl with electric mixer at medium speed until light and fluffy, scraping down side of bowl once. Beat in peanut butter, egg and vanilla, scraping down side of bowl once. Gradually stir in flour mixture with mixing spoon, blending well.

3. Roll heaping tablespoonfuls of dough into 1½-inch balls. Place balls 2 inches apart on ungreased cookie sheets. (If dough is too soft to roll into balls, refrigerate 30 minutes.)

4. Dip table fork into granulated sugar; press criss-cross fashion onto each ball, flattening to ½-inch thickness.

5. Bake 12 minutes or until set. Let cookies stand on cookie sheets 2 minutes. Remove cookies to wire racks; cool completely.

6. Melt semisweet chocolate chips and 1½ teaspoons shortening in top of same double boiler over hot, not boiling, water. Dip one end of each cookie one third the way up; place on waxed paper. Let stand until chocolate is set, about 30 minutes.

7. Melt milk chocolate chips with 1½ teaspoons shortening in top of same double boiler over hot, not boiling, water. Dip opposite end of each cookie one third the way up; place on waxed paper. Let stand until chocolate is set, about 30 minutes. Store cookies between sheets of waxed paper in airtight container at cool room temperature or freeze up to 3 months.

Makes about 2 dozen 3-inch cookies

Irresistible Peanut Butter Cookies

1¼ cups firmly packed light brown sugar
¾ cup creamy peanut butter
½ CRISCO® Stick or ½ cup CRISCO
       all-vegetable shortening
3 tablespoons milk
1 tablespoon vanilla
1 egg
1¾ cups all-purpose flour
¾ teaspoon salt
¾ teaspoon baking soda

1. Heat oven to 375°F. **Place** sheets of foil on countertop for cooling cookies.

2. Combine brown sugar, peanut butter, shortening, milk and vanilla in large bowl. **Beat** at medium speed of electric mixer until well blended. **Add** egg. **Beat** just until blended.

3. Combine flour, salt and baking soda. **Add** to creamed mixture at low speed. **Mix** just until blended.

4. Drop by heaping teaspoonfuls of dough 2 inches apart onto ungreased baking sheet. **Flatten** slightly in criss-cross pattern with tines of fork.

5. Bake one baking sheet at a time at 375°F for 7 to 8 minutes or until set and just beginning to brown. *Do not overbake.* **Cool** 2 minutes on baking sheet. **Remove** cookies to foil to cool completely.

Makes about 3 dozen cookies

Peanut Butter Refrigerator Cookies

2½ cups flour
1 teaspoon baking powder
1 teaspoon baking soda
¼ teaspoon salt
1 cup (2 sticks) MAZOLA® Margarine
1 cup SKIPPY® Creamy or SUPER
   CHUNK® Peanut Butter
1 cup granulated sugar
1 cup packed brown sugar
2 eggs
1 teaspoon vanilla

1. In small bowl combine flour, baking powder, baking soda and salt; set aside.

2. In large bowl with mixer at medium speed, beat margarine and peanut butter until smooth. Beat in both sugars until blended. Beat in eggs and vanilla. Add flour mixture; beat until well blended.

3. Shape dough into two rolls, 1½ inches in diameter. Wrap in plastic wrap; refrigerate until firm.

4. Preheat oven to 350°F. Slice rolls into ¼-inch-thick slices. Place, 2 inches apart, on ungreased cookie sheets.

5. Bake 12 minutes or until lightly browned. Remove; cool completely on wire racks. Store in tightly covered container.   *Makes about 8 dozen cookies*

Cheery Chocolate Teddy Bear Cookies

- 1⅔ cups (10-ounce package) REESE'S₀ Peanut Butter Chips
- 1 cup HERSHEY₀S Semi-Sweet Chocolate Chips
- 2 tablespoons shortening (do *not* use butter, margarine or oil)
- 1 package (20 ounces) chocolate sandwich cookies
- 1 package (10 ounces) teddy bear shaped graham snack crackers

Line trays or cookie sheets with waxed paper. In 2-quart glass measuring cup with handle, combine chips and shortening. Microwave on HIGH (100%) 1½ to 2 minutes or until chips are melted and mixture is smooth when stirred. With fork, dip each cookie into melted chip mixture; gently tap fork on side of cup to remove excess chocolate. Place chocolate-coated cookies on prepared trays; top each cookie with a graham snack cracker. Chill until chocolate is set, about 30 minutes. Store in airtight container in a cool, dry place.   *Makes about 4 dozen cookies*

Chocolate Chip Lollipops

1 package DUNCAN HINES® Chocolate
   Chip Cookie Mix
1 egg
⅓ cup CRISCO® Oil or CRISCO®
   PURITAN® Canola Oil
2 tablespoons water
   Flat ice cream sticks
   Assorted decors

1. Preheat oven to 375°F.

2. Combine cookie mix, egg, oil and water in large
bowl. Stir until thoroughly blended. Shape dough into
32 (1-inch) balls. Place balls 3 inches apart on
ungreased baking sheets. Push ice cream stick into
center of each ball. Flatten each ball with hand to form
round lollipop. Decorate by pressing decors onto
dough.

3. Bake at 375°F for 8 to 9 minutes or until light
golden brown. Cool 1 minute on baking sheets.
Remove to cooling racks. Cool completely. Store in
airtight container.   *Makes 2½ to 3 dozen cookies*

Tip: For best results, use shiny baking sheets for
baking cookies. Dark baking sheets cause cookie
bottoms to become too brown.

Surprise Cookies

2 squares (1 ounce each) semisweet
   baking chocolate, coarsely chopped
1¼ cups all-purpose flour
½ teaspoon baking powder
¼ teaspoon salt
½ cup butter or margarine, softened
½ cup sugar
1 large egg
1 teaspoon vanilla extract
   Fillings as desired: maraschino cherries
      (well drained) or candied cherries;
      chocolate mint candies, broken in
      half; white baking bar, cut into
      chunks; thick milk chocolate candy
      bar, cut into chunks or semi-sweet
      chocolate chunks; raspberry jam or
      apricot preserves
   Nonpareils (optional)

1. Preheat oven to 350°F. Grease mini-muffin cups.

2. Melt 2 squares chocolate in heavy small saucepan over low heat, stirring constantly; set aside.

3. Combine flour, baking powder and salt in small bowl. Beat butter and sugar in large bowl with electric mixer at medium speed until light and fluffy, scraping down side of bowl once. Beat in egg and vanilla, scraping down side of bowl once. Gradually beat in melted chocolate. Gradually add flour mixture. Beat at low speed, scraping down side of bowl once.

4. Drop level teaspoonfuls of dough into prepared muffin cups. Smooth down dough and form small indentation with back of teaspoon. Fill as desired with assorted filling ingredients. Top with heaping teaspoonful of dough, smoothing top lightly with back of spoon. Sprinkle tops with nonpareils, if desired.

5. Bake 15 to 17 minutes until centers of cookies are set. Remove pan to wire rack; cool completely before removing cookies from pan. Store tightly covered at room temperature. (These cookies do not freeze well.)

Makes 1 dozen cookies

Luscious Cookie Drops Made with MILKY WAY® Bars

3 MILKY WAY® Bars (2.15 ounces each), chopped, divided
2 tablespoons milk
½ cup butter or margarine, softened
⅓ cup packed light brown sugar
1 egg
½ teaspoon vanilla extract
1⅔ cups all-purpose flour
½ teaspoon baking soda
¼ teaspoon salt
½ cup chopped walnuts

Preheat oven to 350°F. Stir 1 MILKY WAY® Bar with milk in small saucepan over low heat until melted and smooth; cool. In large bowl, beat butter and brown sugar until creamy. Beat in egg, vanilla and melted MILKY WAY® Bar mixture. Combine flour, baking soda and salt in small bowl. Stir into chocolate mixture. Add remaining chopped MILKY WAY® Bars and nuts; stir gently. Drop dough by rounded teaspoonfuls onto ungreased cookie sheets.

Bake 12 to 15 minutes or until cookies are just firm to the touch. Cool on wire racks.

Makes about 2 dozen cookies

Chocolate Malted Cookies

¾ cup firmly packed light brown sugar
⅔ CRISCO® Stick or ⅔ cup CRISCO
      all-vegetable shortening
1 teaspoon vanilla
1 egg
1¾ cups all-purpose flour
½ cup malted milk powder
⅓ cup unsweetened cocoa powder
¾ teaspoon baking soda
½ teaspoon salt
2 cups malted milk balls, broken into
      large pieces*

1. Heat oven to 375°F. **Place** sheets of foil on countertop for cooling cookies.

2. Place brown sugar, shortening and vanilla in large bowl. **Beat** at medium speed of electric mixer until well blended. **Add** egg; beat well.

3. Combine flour, malted milk powder, cocoa, baking soda and salt. **Add** to shortening mixture; beat at low speed just until blended. **Stir** in malted milk pieces.

4. Drop dough by rounded measuring tablespoonfuls 2 inches apart onto ungreased baking sheet.

5. Bake one baking sheet at a time at 375°F for 7 to 9 minutes or until cookies are set. *Do not overbake.* **Cool** 2 minutes on baking sheet. **Remove** cookies to foil to cool completely.   *Makes about 3 dozen cookies*

*Place malted milk balls in heavy resealable plastic bag; break malted milk balls with rolling pin or back of heavy spoon.

Chocolate Thumbprint Cookies

½ cup (1 stick) butter or margarine,
  softened
⅔ cup sugar
1 egg, separated
2 tablespoons milk
1 teaspoon vanilla extract
1 cup all-purpose flour
⅓ cup HERSHEY'S Cocoa
¼ teaspoon salt
1 cup chopped nuts
  Vanilla Filling (recipe follows)
26 HERSHEY'S KISSES® Milk Chocolates
  or HERSHEY'S HUGS® Chocolates
  or pecan halves or candied cherry
  halves

In medium bowl, beat butter, sugar, egg yolk, milk and vanilla until light and fluffy. Stir together flour, cocoa and salt; gradually add to butter mixture, beating until blended. Cover; refrigerate dough at least 1 hour or until firm enough to handle. Heat oven to 350°F. Lightly grease cookie sheet. Shape dough into 1-inch balls. With fork, beat egg white slightly. Dip each ball into egg white; roll in nuts. Place on prepared cookie sheet. Press thumb gently in center of each cookie.

Bake cookies 10 to 12 minutes or until set. Meanwhile, prepare Vanilla Filling. Remove wrappers from chocolate pieces. Remove cookies from cookie sheet to wire rack; cool 5 minutes. Spoon about ¼ teaspoon prepared filling into each thumbprint. Gently press chocolate piece onto top of each cookie. Cool completely.   *Makes about 2 dozen cookies*

Vanilla Filling

   ½   **cup powdered sugar**
   1   **tablespoon butter or margarine,**
        softened
   2   **teaspoons milk**
   ¼   **teaspoon vanilla extract**

In small bowl, combine powdered sugar, butter, milk and vanilla; beat until smooth.

Cowboy Macaroons

¾ BUTTER FLAVOR* CRISCO® Stick or
  ¾ cup BUTTER FLAVOR CRISCO
  all-vegetable shortening
1¼ cups firmly packed light brown sugar
1 egg
⅓ cup milk
1½ teaspoons vanilla
1½ cups quick oats, uncooked
1½ cups corn flakes
1 cup all-purpose flour
½ teaspoon baking soda
½ teaspoon salt
¼ teaspoon cinnamon
1 cup coarsely chopped walnuts
¾ cup finely chopped pecans
¾ cup flake coconut
⅓ cup maraschino cherries, cut into
  quarters (optional)

*Butter Flavor Crisco is artificially flavored.

1. Heat oven to 375°F. **Grease** baking sheets with
shortening. **Place** sheets of foil on countertop for
cooling cookies.

2. Combine shortening, brown sugar, egg, milk and
vanilla in large bowl. **Beat** at medium speed of electric
mixer until well blended.

3. Combine oats, corn flakes, flour, baking soda, salt and cinnamon. **Mix** into shortening mixture at low speed just until blended. **Stir** in nuts, coconut and cherries.

4. Form dough into 1-inch balls. **Place** 2 inches apart onto prepared baking sheets.

5. Bake one baking sheet at a time at 375°F for 10 to 12 minutes or until lightly browned. *Do not overbake.* **Cool** 2 minutes on baking sheets. **Remove** cookies to foil to cool completely.

Makes about 3 dozen cookies

KELLOGG'S® Corn Flake Macaroons

    4   egg whites
    ¼   teaspoon cream of tartar
    1   teaspoon vanilla
    1⅓ cups sugar
    1   cup chopped pecans
    1   cup shredded coconut
    3   cups KELLOGG'S CORN FLAKES®
        cereal
        Vegetable cooking spray

1. In large mixing bowl, beat egg whites until foamy. Beat in cream of tartar and vanilla. Gradually add sugar, beating until stiff and glossy. Fold in pecans, coconut and KELLOGG'S CORN FLAKES® cereal. Drop by rounded measuring-tablespoon onto cookie sheets coated with cooking spray.

2. Bake about 15 minutes or until lightly browned. Remove immediately from baking sheets. Cool on wire racks.   *Makes about 3 dozen cookies*

Merry Macaroons: Fold in ½ cup crushed peppermint candy with pecans and coconut.

Crispie Treats

- **4 cups miniature marshmallows**
- **½ cup peanut butter**
- **¼ cup margarine**
- **⅛ teaspoon salt**
- **4 cups crisped rice cereal**
- **1½ cups "M & M's"® Plain or Peanut Chocolate Candies**

Melt together marshmallows, peanut butter, margarine and salt in large, heavy saucepan over low heat, stirring occasionally, until smooth. Pour over combined cereal and candies, tossing lightly until thoroughly coated. With greased fingers, gently shape into 1½-inch balls. Place on waxed paper; cool at room temperature until set. *Makes about 3 dozen cookies*

Variation: After cereal mixture is thoroughly coated, press lightly into greased 13×9-inch baking pan. Cool thoroughly; cut into bars. Makes about 32 bars.

Toffee Tassies

½ cup margarine or butter
1 (3-ounce) package cream cheese, softened
1 cup all-purpose flour
¼ cup ground pecans
¾ cup packed brown sugar
1 egg
1 tablespoon margarine or butter, melted
½ cup chopped pecans
½ cup HEATH® Bits

For pastry, in medium mixing bowl beat ½ cup margarine or butter and cream cheese until thoroughly combined. Stir in flour and ground pecans. Press a rounded teaspoon of pastry evenly into the bottom and up sides of 24 ungreased 1¾-inch miniature muffin cups. Set aside.

For filling, beat together brown sugar, egg and 1 tablespoon melted margarine or butter in small mixing bowl. Stir in chopped pecans. Spoon 1 teaspoon filling into each pastry-lined cup. Sprinkle about 1 teaspoon HEATH® Bits over filling. Bake in 325°F oven about 30 minutes or until pastry is golden and filling is puffed. Cool slightly in pans on wire racks. Remove and cool completely on wire racks.   *Makes 24 tassies*

Oatmeal Cookies

1 cup all-purpose flour
1 teaspoon baking powder
½ teaspoon baking soda
½ teaspoon salt
¼ cup MOTT'S® Cinnamon Apple Sauce
2 tablespoons margarine
½ cup granulated sugar
½ cup firmly packed light brown sugar
1 egg
1 teaspoon vanilla extract
1⅓ cups uncooked rolled oats
½ cup raisins (optional)

1. Preheat oven to 375°F. Spray cookie sheet with nonstick cooking spray.

2. In small bowl, combine flour, baking powder, baking soda and salt.

3. In large bowl, place apple sauce. Cut in margarine with pastry blender or fork until margarine breaks into pea-sized pieces. Add granulated sugar, brown sugar, egg and vanilla; stir until well blended.

4. Add flour mixture to apple sauce mixture; stir until well blended. Fold in oats and raisins, if desired.

5. Drop rounded teaspoonfuls of dough 2 inches apart onto prepared cookie sheet.

6. Bake 10 to 12 minutes or until lightly browned. Cool 5 minutes on cookie sheet. Remove to wire rack; cool completely.   *Makes 3 dozen cookies*

Giant Oatmeal Cookies

1   cup firmly packed brown sugar
¾   cup (1½ sticks) margarine or butter,
      softened
2   eggs
1   teaspoon vanilla
1¼ cups all-purpose flour
½   teaspoon baking soda
½   teaspoon salt (optional)
2½ cups QUAKER® Oats (Quick or Old
      Fashioned), uncooked
1   (6-ounce) package semisweet chocolate
      pieces (1 cup)
½   cup chopped nuts

Heat oven to 350°F. Lightly grease 2 large cookie
sheets. Beat sugar and margarine until light and fluffy.
Blend in eggs and vanilla. Add combined flour, baking
soda, salt and oats; mix well. Stir in chocolate pieces
and nuts. Divide dough in half. Press each half into
circle about ¾ inch thick on prepared cookie sheets.
Bake 17 to 20 minutes or until lightly browned. Cool 5
minutes on cookie sheets; remove to wire racks. Cool
completely. Cut into wedges to serve.

Makes 2 giant cookies

Variation: Drop dough by rounded tablespoonfuls onto
greased cookie sheets. Bake 10 to 12 minutes. Makes
about 3 dozen cookies.

Whole-Wheat Oatmeal Cookies

1 **cup whole-wheat flour**
1 **teaspoon ground cinnamon**
1 **teaspoon baking powder**
½ **teaspoon baking soda**
½ **teaspoon salt**
1 **cup packed light brown sugar**
¼ **cup unsweetened applesauce**
2 **egg whites**
2 **tablespoons margarine**
1½ **teaspoons vanilla extract**
1⅓ **cups rolled oats, uncooked**
½ **cup raisins**

1. Preheat oven to 375°F. Lightly spray cookie sheets with nonstick cooking spray.

2. Combine flour, cinnamon, baking powder, baking soda and salt in medium bowl; mix well. Combine brown sugar, applesauce, egg whites, margarine and vanilla in large bowl. Mix until small crumbs form. Add flour mixture; blend well. Blend in oats and raisins.

3. Drop by rounded teaspoonfuls onto prepared cookie sheets, 2 inches apart. Bake 10 to 12 minutes until golden brown. Remove to wire racks; cool completely. Store tightly covered. *Makes 3½ dozen cookies*

Chewy Oatmeal Cookies

¾ **BUTTER FLAVOR* CRISCO® Stick or**
   ¾ cup BUTTER FLAVOR CRISCO
   all-vegetable shortening
1¼ **cups firmly packed light brown sugar**
1 **egg**
⅓ **cup milk**
1½ **teaspoons vanilla**
3 **cups quick cooking oats, uncooked**
1 **cup all-purpose flour**
½ **teaspoon baking soda**
½ **teaspoon salt**
¼ **teaspoon ground cinnamon**
1 **cup raisins**
1 **cup coarsely chopped walnuts**

*Butter Flavor Crisco is artificially flavored.

1. Heat oven to 375°F. **Grease** baking sheets with shortening. **Place** sheets of foil on countertop for cooling cookies.

2. Combine shortening, brown sugar, egg, milk and vanilla in large bowl. **Beat** at medium speed of electric mixer until well blended.

3. Combine oats, flour, baking soda, salt and cinnamon. **Mix** into creamed mixture at low speed just until blended. **Stir** in raisins and nuts.

4. Drop rounded tablespoonfuls of dough 2 inches apart onto baking sheet.

5. Bake one baking sheet at a time at 375°F for 10 to 12 minutes or until lightly browned. *Do not overbake.* **Cool** 2 minutes on baking sheet. **Remove** cookies to foil to cool completely.

Makes about 2½ dozen cookies

Brownie Sandwich Cookies

BROWNIE COOKIES
> 1 **package DUNCAN HINES® Double Fudge Brownie Mix**
> 1 **egg**
> 3 **tablespoons water**
>   **Sugar**

FILLING
> 1 **container (16 ounces) DUNCAN HINES® Creamy Homestyle Cream Cheese Frosting**
>   **Red food coloring (optional)**
> ½ **cup semisweet mini chocolate chips**

1. Preheat oven to 375°F. Grease cookie sheets.

2. For brownie cookies, combine brownie mix, fudge packet from Mix, egg and water in large bowl. Stir until well blended, about 50 strokes. Shape dough into 50 (1-inch) balls. Place 2 inches apart on prepared cookie sheets. Grease bottom of drinking glass; dip in sugar. Press gently to flatten 1 cookie to ⅜-inch thickness. Repeat with remaining cookies. Bake at 375°F for 6 to 7 minutes or until set. Cool 1 minute on cookie sheets. Remove to cooling racks. Cool completely.

3. For filling, tint frosting with red food coloring, if desired. Stir in chocolate chips.

4. To assemble, spread 1 tablespoon frosting on bottom of one cookie; top with second cookie. Press together to make sandwich cookie. Repeat with remaining cookies. Store in airtight container.

Makes 25 sandwich cookies

Low Fat Chocolate Chip Cookies

1 cup Prune Purée (page 280) or
  prepared prune butter
¾ cup granulated sugar
¾ cup packed brown sugar
3 egg whites
1 teaspoon vanilla
2¼ cups all-purpose flour
1 teaspoon baking soda
1 teaspoon salt
2 cups (12 ounces) semisweet chocolate
  chips

Preheat oven to 375°F. Coat baking sheets with
vegetable cooking spray. In large bowl, beat prune
purée, sugars, egg whites and vanilla until well
blended. In small bowl, combine flour, baking soda and
salt; mix into prune purée mixture until well blended.
Stir in chocolate chips. Drop tablespoonfuls of dough
onto prepared baking sheets, spacing 2 inches apart;
flatten slightly. Bake in center of oven about 10
minutes until lightly browned around edges. Remove
from baking sheets to wire racks to cool completely.

Makes about 60 (2¼-inch) cookies

Favorite recipe from **California Prune Board**

Chocolate Chip Ice Cream Sandwiches

- 1¼ cups firmly packed light brown sugar
- ¾ BUTTER FLAVOR* CRISCO® Stick or
  ¾ cup BUTTER FLAVOR CRISCO
  all-vegetable shortening
- 2 tablespoons milk
- 1 tablespoon vanilla
- 1 egg
- 1¾ cups all-purpose flour
- 1 teaspoon salt
- ¾ teaspoon baking soda
- 1 cup semisweet chocolate chips
- 1 cup chopped pecans
- 2 pints ice cream, any flavor

*Butter Flavor Crisco is artificially flavored.

1. Heat oven to 375°F. **Place** sheets of foil on countertop for cooling cookies.

2. Place brown sugar, shortening, milk and vanilla in large bowl. **Beat** at medium speed of electric mixer until well blended. **Add** egg; beat well.

3. Combine flour, salt and baking soda. **Add** to shortening mixture; beat at low speed just until blended. **Stir** in chocolate chips and pecans.

4. Measure ¼ cup dough; shape into ball. **Repeat** with remaining dough. **Place** balls 4 inches apart on ungreased baking sheets. **Flatten** balls into 3-inch circles.

5. Bake one baking sheet at a time at 375°F for 10 to 12 minutes or until cookies are lightly browned. *Do not overbake.* **Cool** 2 minutes on baking sheet. **Remove** cookies to foil to cool completely.

6. Remove ice cream from freezer to soften slightly. **Measure** ½ cup ice cream; spread onto bottom of one cookie. **Cover** with flat side of second cookie. **Wrap** sandwich in plastic wrap. **Place** in freezer. **Repeat** with remaining cookies and ice cream.

Makes about 10 ice cream sandwiches

Note: Chocolate Chip Ice Cream Sandwiches should be eaten within two days. After two days, cookies will absorb moisture and become soggy. If longer storage is needed, make and freeze cookies, but assemble ice cream sandwiches within two days of serving.

Lemon Pecan Cookies

1⅔ cups (10-ounce package) HERSHEY'S
    Premier White Chips, divided
2¼ cups all-purpose flour
¾ cup sugar
2 eggs
¾ teaspoon baking soda
½ teaspoon freshly grated lemon peel
¼ teaspoon lemon extract
½ cup (1 stick) butter or margarine
¾ cup chopped pecans
    Lemon Drizzle (recipe follows)

Heat oven to 350°F. Reserve 2 tablespoons white chips
for drizzle. In large bowl, place flour, sugar, eggs,
baking soda, lemon peel and lemon extract. In medium
microwave-safe bowl, place remaining white chips and
butter. Microwave at HIGH (100%) 1 minute; stir. If
necessary, microwave at HIGH an additional 15
seconds at a time, stirring after each heating, just until
chips and butter are melted when stirred. Add white
chip mixture to flour mixture; beat until blended. Stir
in pecans. Drop dough by rounded teaspoons onto
ungreased cookie sheet. Bake 9 to 11 minutes or until
very slightly golden around edges. Remove from cookie
sheet to wire rack. Cool completely. Prepare Lemon
Drizzle; lightly drizzle over cookies.

Makes about 3½ dozen cookies

Lemon Drizzle

2   tablespoons HERSHEY₂S Premier
       White Chips (reserved from cookies)
½   **teaspoon shortening (do *not* use butter,
       margarine or oil)**
       Yellow food color
       Lemon extract

In small microwave-safe bowl, place reserved white
chips and shortening. Microwave at HIGH (100%) 30
seconds; stir. If necessary, microwave at HIGH an
additional 15 seconds at a time, stirring after each
heating, just until chips are melted when stirred. Stir
in a few drops of food color and a few drops lemon
extract, if desired.

Lemonade Cookies

1¼ cups granulated sugar
¾ **BUTTER FLAVOR* CRISCO® Stick or
   ¾ cup BUTTER FLAVOR CRISCO
   all-vegetable shortening**
2 tablespoons freshly squeezed lemon
   juice
1 tablespoon grated lemon peel
1 teaspoon vanilla
1 teaspoon lemon extract
1 egg
1¾ cups all-purpose flour
¾ teaspoon baking soda
½ teaspoon salt
½ cup flaked coconut (optional)

*Butter Flavor Crisco is artificially flavored.

1. Heat oven to 375°F. **Place** sheets of foil on countertop for cooling cookies.

2. Place sugar, shortening, lemon juice, lemon peel, vanilla and lemon extract in large bowl. **Beat** at medium speed of electric mixer until well blended. **Add** egg; beat well.

3. Combine flour, baking soda and salt. **Add** to shortening mixture; beat at low speed just until blended.

4. Drop dough by rounded measuring tablespoonfuls 3 inches apart onto ungreased baking sheets. **Sprinkle** tops with coconut, if desired.

5. Bake one baking sheet at a time at 375°F for 8 to 10 minutes or until cookies are set and edges are lightly browned. (Watch closely; do not allow coconut to burn.) *Do not overbake.* **Cool** 2 minutes on baking sheet. **Remove** cookies to foil to cool completely.

Makes about 3 dozen cookies

Especially

ELEGANT

Chocolate-Dipped Almond Horns

- 1 can SOLO® Almond Paste
- 3 egg whites
- ½ cup superfine sugar
- ½ teaspoon almond extract
- ¼ cup plus 2 tablespoons all-purpose flour
- ½ cup sliced almonds
- 5 squares (1 ounce each) semisweet chocolate, melted and cooled

Preheat oven to 350°F. Grease 2 cookie sheets. Break almond paste into small pieces and place in medium bowl or food processor container. Add egg whites, sugar and almond extract. Beat with electric mixer or process until mixture is very smooth. Add flour and beat or process until blended.

Spoon almond mixture into pastry bag fitted with ½-inch (#8) plain tip. Pipe mixture into 5- or 6-inch crescent shapes on prepared cookie sheets, about 1½ inches apart. Sprinkle with sliced almonds.

Bake 13 to 15 minutes or until edges are golden brown. Cool on cookie sheets on wire racks 2 minutes. Remove from cookie sheets and cool completely on wire racks. Dip ends of cookies in melted chocolate and place on aluminum foil. Let stand until chocolate is set.   *Makes about 16 cookies*

Almond Hearts

1 **package DUNCAN HINES® Golden Sugar Cookie Mix**
¾ **cup ground almonds**
2 **egg yolks**
⅓ **cup CRISCO® Oil or CRISCO® PURITAN® Canola Oil**
1½ **tablespoons water**
14 **ounces (6 cubes) vanilla flavored candy coating**
Pink candy coating, for garnish

1. Preheat oven to 375°F.

2. Combine cookie mix, ground almonds, egg yolks, oil and water in large bowl. Stir until thoroughly blended.

3. Divide dough in half. Roll half the dough between 2 sheets of waxed paper into 11-inch circle. Slide onto flat surface. Refrigerate about 15 minutes. Repeat with remaining dough. Loosen top sheet of waxed paper from dough. Turn over and remove second sheet of waxed paper. Cut dough with 2½-inch heart cookie cutter. Place cut-outs 2 inches apart on ungreased cookie sheets. (Roll leftover cookie dough to ⅛-inch thickness between sheets of waxed paper. Chill before cutting.) Repeat cutting with remaining dough circle. Bake at 375°F for 6 to 8 minutes or until light golden brown. Cool 1 minute on cookie sheets. Remove to cooling racks. Cool completely.

4. Place vanilla candy coating in 1-quart saucepan on low heat; stir until melted and smooth. Dip half of one heart cookie into candy coating. Allow excess to drip back into pan. Place cookie on waxed paper. Repeat with remaining cookies. Place pink candy coating in small saucepan on low heat. Stir until melted and smooth. Pour into pastry bag fitted with small writing tip. Decorate tops of cookies as desired. Allow candy coating to set before storing between layers of waxed paper in airtight container.

Makes about 5 dozen cookies

Chocolate-Dipped Cinnamon Thins

1¼ cups all-purpose flour
1½ teaspoons ground cinnamon
¼ teaspoon salt
1 cup unsalted butter, softened
1 cup powdered sugar
1 large egg
1 teaspoon vanilla extract
4 ounces broken bittersweet chocolate
   candy bar

1. Combine flour, cinnamon and salt in small bowl. Beat butter in large bowl with electric mixer at medium speed until light and fluffy, scraping down side of bowl once. Add sugar; beat well. Add egg and vanilla; beat well, scraping down side of bowl once. Gradually add flour mixture. Beat at low speed, scraping down side of bowl occasionally.

2. Place dough on sheet of waxed paper. Using waxed paper to hold dough, roll it back and forth to form a log about 12 inches long and 2½ inches wide.

3. Securely wrap log in plastic wrap. Refrigerate at least 2 hours or until firm. (Log may be frozen up to 3 months; thaw in refrigerator before baking.)

4. Preheat oven to 350°F. Cut dough with long, sharp knife into ¼-inch-thick slices. Place 2 inches apart on ungreased cookie sheets.

5. Bake 10 minutes or until set. Let cookies stand on cookie sheets 2 minutes. Remove cookies with spatula to wire racks; cool completely.

6. Melt chocolate in 1-cup glass measure set in bowl of very hot water, stirring twice. Dip each cookie into chocolate, coating 1 inch up sides. Let excess chocolate drip back into cup.

7. Transfer to wire racks or waxed paper; let stand at cool room temperature about 40 minutes until chocolate is set. Store between sheets of waxed paper at cool room temperature or in refrigerator. (These cookies do not freeze well.)

Makes about 2 dozen cookies

Double-Dipped Hazelnut Crisps

¾ cup semisweet chocolate chips
1¼ cups all-purpose flour
¾ cup powdered sugar
⅔ cup whole hazelnuts, toasted, hulled
   and pulverized*
¼ teaspoon instant espresso powder
   Dash salt
½ cup butter or margarine, softened
2 teaspoons vanilla extract
4 squares (1 ounce each) bittersweet or
   semisweet chocolate
2 teaspoons shortening, divided
4 ounces white chocolate

*To pulverize hazelnuts, place in food processor or blender. Process until thoroughly ground with a dry, not pasty, texture.

1. Preheat oven to 350°F. Lightly grease cookie sheets or line with parchment paper.

2. Melt chocolate chips in top of double boiler over hot, not boiling, water. Remove from heat; cool.

3. Blend flour, sugar, hazelnuts, espresso powder and salt in large bowl. Blend in butter, melted chocolate and vanilla until dough is stiff but smooth. (If dough is too soft to handle, cover and refrigerate until firm.)

4. Roll out dough, ¼ at a time, to ⅛-inch thickness on lightly floured surface. Cut out with 2-inch scalloped round cutters. Place 2 inches apart on prepared cookie sheets.

5. Bake 8 minutes or until not quite firm. (Cookies should not brown. They will puff up during baking and then fall again.) Remove to wire racks to cool.

6. Place bittersweet chocolate and 1 teaspoon shortening in small bowl. Place bowl over hot water; stir until chocolate is melted and smooth. Dip cookies, 1 at a time, halfway into bittersweet chocolate. Place on waxed paper; refrigerate until chocolate is set.

7. Repeat melting process with white chocolate and remaining 1 teaspoon shortening. Dip other halves of cookies into white chocolate; refrigerate until set. Store cookies in airtight container in cool place. (If cookies are frozen, chocolate may discolor.)

Makes about 4 dozen cookies

Chocolate-Dipped Brandy Snaps

½ **cup (1 stick) butter**
½ **cup granulated sugar**
⅓ **cup dark corn syrup**
½ **teaspoon ground cinnamon**
¼ **teaspoon ground ginger**
1 **cup all-purpose flour**
2 **teaspoons brandy**
1 **cup (6 ounces) NESTLÉ® TOLL HOUSE® Semi-Sweet Chocolate Morsels**
1 **tablespoon shortening**
⅓ **cup finely chopped nuts**

MELT butter, sugar, corn syrup, cinnamon and ginger in medium heavy-duty saucepan over low heat, stirring until smooth. Remove from heat; stir in flour and brandy. Drop by rounded teaspoon onto ungreased baking sheets about 3 inches apart, baking no more than six at a time.

BAKE in preheated 300°F. oven for 10 to 14 minutes or until deep caramel color. Cool for 10 seconds. Remove from baking sheets and immediately roll around wooden spoon handle; cool completely on wire racks.

MICROWAVE morsels and shortening in medium microwave-safe bowl on HIGH (100% power) for 45 seconds; stir. Microwave at 10- to 20-second intervals, stirring until smooth. Dip cookies halfway in melted chocolate; shake off excess. Sprinkle with nuts; set on waxed paper-lined baking sheets. Chill for 10 minutes or until chocolate is set. Store in airtight container in refrigerator.   *Makes about 3 dozen cookies*

Brandy Lace Cookies

¼ **cup sugar**

¼ **cup (½ stick) MAZOLA® Margarine**

¼ **cup KARO® Light or Dark Corn Syrup**

½ **cup flour**

¼ **cup very finely chopped pecans or walnuts**

2 **tablespoons brandy**

Melted white and/or semisweet chocolate (optional)

1. Preheat oven to 350°F. Lightly grease and flour cookie sheets.

2. In small saucepan combine sugar, margarine and corn syrup. Bring to boil over medium heat, stirring constantly. Remove from heat. Stir in flour, pecans and brandy. Drop 12 evenly spaced half teaspoonfuls of batter onto prepared cookie sheets.

3. Bake 6 minutes or until golden. Cool 1 to 2 minutes or until cookies can be lifted but are still warm and pliable; remove with spatula. Curl around handle of wooden spoon; slide off when crisp. If cookies harden before curling, return to oven to soften.

4. If desired, drizzle with melted chocolate.

Makes 4 to 5 dozen cookies

Apricot-Filled Pastries

Apricot Filling (recipe follows)
2¼ cups flour
⅔ cup sugar
1 cup (2 sticks) MAZOLA® Margarine or
   butter
2 egg yolks, lightly beaten
½ cup sour cream
   Confectioners sugar

1. Prepare Apricot Filling; set aside.

2. In large bowl combine flour and sugar. With pastry blender or 2 knives, cut in margarine until mixture resembles coarse crumbs. Stir in egg yolks and sour cream until mixed. Turn onto floured surface; knead just until smooth. Divide dough into quarters. Cover; refrigerate 20 minutes.

3. Preheat oven to 375°F.

4. On floured pastry cloth with stockinette-covered rolling pin, roll one piece of dough at a time into 10-inch square. (Keep remaining dough refrigerated.) Cut dough into 2-inch squares.

5. Place ½ teaspoon Apricot Filling diagonally across each square. Moisten 2 opposite corners with water; fold over filling, overlapping slightly. Place on ungreased cookie sheets. Bake 10 to 12 minutes or until edges are lightly browned. Cool on wire racks.

6. Just before serving, sprinkle with confectioners sugar. Store in tightly covered container up to 3 weeks.

Makes about 8 dozen pastries

Apricot Filling: In 1-quart saucepan bring 1 cup dried apricots and 1 cup water to boil over medium-high heat. Reduce heat; cover and simmer 5 minutes. Drain. Place apricots and ½ cup KARO® Light Corn Syrup in blender container or food processor. Cover and blend on high speed 2 minutes or until smooth. Cool completely.   *Makes about 1½ cups filling*

Walnut Jam Crescents

⅔ **cup butter or margarine**
1⅓ **cups all-purpose flour**
½ **cup dairy sour cream**
⅔ **cup raspberry jam or orange marmalade, divided**
⅔ **cup DIAMOND® Walnuts, finely chopped, divided**

Preheat oven to 350°F. In medium bowl, cut butter into flour until mixture resembles fine crumbs. Add sour cream; mix until stiff dough is formed. Divide dough in half. Shape each half into a ball; flatten slightly. Wrap balls in waxed paper; chill well. Working with one half of dough at a time, roll dough into 11-inch round on lightly floured pastry cloth or board. Spread with ⅓ cup jam; sprinkle with ⅓ cup walnuts. Cut into quarters; cut each quarter into three wedges. Roll up, one at a time, starting from outer edge; place on lightly greased cookie sheets. Repeat with remaining half of dough. Bake 25 to 30 minutes or until lightly browned. Remove to wire racks to cool.
Makes about 2 dozen crescents

English Thumbprint Cookies

- 1 **cup pecan pieces**
- 1¼ **cups all-purpose flour**
- ¼ **teaspoon salt**
- ½ **cup butter, softened**
- ½ **cup firmly packed light brown sugar**
- 1 **teaspoon vanilla extract**
- 1 **large egg, separated**
  Seedless raspberry or strawberry jam

1. Preheat oven to 350°F. To toast pecans, spread on baking sheet. Bake 8 to 10 minutes until golden brown, stirring frequently. Remove pecans from baking sheet; cool completely.

2. Place cooled pecans in food processor. Process until finely chopped; transfer to shallow bowl.

3. Combine flour and salt in medium bowl. Beat butter and brown sugar in large bowl with electric mixer until light and fluffy, scraping down side of bowl once. Beat in vanilla and egg yolk. Gradually beat in flour mixture, scraping down side of bowl once.

4. Beat egg white with fork until frothy. Roll dough into 1-inch balls. Roll balls in egg white; roll in nuts to cover.

5. Place balls 2 inches apart on ungreased cookie sheets. Press a deep indentation in center of each ball with thumb.

6. Bake 8 minutes or until set. Remove from oven; fill each indentation with ¼ teaspoon jam. Return to oven; bake 8 to 10 minutes until lightly brown.

7. Remove cookies to wire racks; cool completely. Store tightly covered at room temperature or freeze up to 3 months.   *Makes about 2½ dozen cookies*

Chocolate Raspberry Thumbprints

   1½ **cups butter or margarine, softened**
   1 **cup sugar**
   1 **egg**
   1 **teaspoon vanilla extract**
   3 **cups all-purpose flour**
   ¼ **cup unsweetened cocoa**
   ½ **teaspoon salt**
   1 **cup (6 ounces) semisweet mini chocolate chips**
   ⅔ **cup raspberry preserves**
     Powdered sugar (optional)

Preheat oven to 350°F. Grease cookie sheets. Beat butter and sugar in large bowl. Beat in egg and vanilla until light and fluffy. Mix in flour, cocoa and salt until well blended. Stir in chocolate chips. Roll level tablespoonfuls of dough into balls. Place 2 inches apart onto prepared cookie sheets. Make deep indentation in center of each ball with thumb.

Bake 12 to 15 minutes until just set. Cool 2 minutes on cookie sheets. Remove to wire racks; cool completely. Fill centers with raspberry preserves and sprinkle with powdered sugar, if desired. Store between layers of waxed paper in airtight containers at room temperature.   *Makes about 4½ dozen cookies*

Chocolate Thumbprints

COOKIES

- 1½ cups firmly packed light brown sugar
- ⅔ CRISCO® Stick or ⅔ cup CRISCO all-vegetable shortening
- 1 tablespoon water
- 1 teaspoon vanilla
- 2 eggs
- 1½ cups all-purpose flour
- ⅓ cup unsweetened baking cocoa
- ½ teaspoon salt
- ¼ teaspoon baking soda
- ½ cup miniature chocolate chips

PEANUT BUTTER CREAM FILLING

- ⅓ cup creamy peanut butter
- 2 tablespoons BUTTER FLAVOR* CRISCO** all-vegetable shortening
- 1 cup confectioners' sugar
- 2 tablespoons milk
- ½ teaspoon vanilla

*Butter Flavor Crisco is artificially flavored.

**Crisco all-vegetable shortening can be substituted for Butter Flavor Crisco.

1. Heat oven to 375°F.

2. *For cookies,* combine brown sugar, ⅔ cup shortening, water and 1 teaspoon vanilla in large bowl. **Beat** at medium speed of electric mixer until well blended. **Beat** in eggs until well blended.

3. Combine flour, cocoa, salt and baking soda in medium bowl. **Mix** into shortening mixture at low speed just until blended. **Stir** in chocolate chips.

4. Shape dough into 1-inch balls. **Place** 2 inches apart on ungreased baking sheets. **Press** thumb gently into center of each cookie.

5. Bake at 375°F for 7 to 9 minutes or until set. **Press** centers again with small measuring spoon. **Cool** 2 minutes on baking sheets. **Remove** to wire racks to cool completely.

6. *For peanut butter cream filling,* combine peanut butter and 2 tablespoons shortening in medium bowl. **Stir** with spoon until blended. **Add** confectioners' sugar. **Stir** well. **Add** milk and ½ teaspoon vanilla. **Stir** until smooth. **Spoon** into centers of cookies.

Makes about 3 dozen cookies

Choco-Caramel Delights

½ cup (1 stick) butter or margarine,
  softened
⅔ cup sugar
1 egg, separated
2 tablespoons milk
1 teaspoon vanilla extract
1 cup all-purpose flour
⅓ cup HERSHEY₀S Cocoa
¼ teaspoon salt
1 cup finely chopped pecans
  Caramel Filling (recipe follows)
½ cup HERSHEY₀S Semi-Sweet
  Chocolate Chips
1 teaspoon shortening (do *not* use butter,
  margarine or oil)

In medium bowl, beat butter, sugar, egg yolk, milk and
vanilla until blended. Stir together flour, cocoa and
salt; add to butter mixture, beating until well blended.
Refrigerate dough about 1 hour or until firm enough
to handle. Heat oven to 350°F. Lightly grease cookie
sheet. Beat egg white slightly. Shape dough into 1-inch
balls. Dip each ball into egg white; roll in pecans to
coat. Place on prepared cookie sheet. Press thumb
gently in center of each ball. Bake 10 to 12 minutes or
until set. Meanwhile, prepare Caramel Filling. Remove
cookies from oven; carefully press center of each
cookie again with thumb to make indentation.
Immediately spoon about ½ teaspoon Caramel Filling
in center of each cookie. Carefully remove from cookie
sheet. Cool completely.

In small microwave-safe bowl, place chocolate chips and shortening. Microwave at HIGH (100%) 1 minute or until smooth when stirred. Place wax paper under wire rack with cookies. Drizzle chocolate mixture over top of cookies. *Makes 2 dozen cookies*

Caramel Filling: Remove wrappers from 14 caramels. In small saucepan, combine caramels and 3 tablespoons whipping cream. Cook over low heat, stirring frequently, until caramels are melted and mixture is smooth.

Almond Toffee Triangles

Bar Cookie Crust (page 252)
⅓ cup KARO® Light or Dark Corn Syrup
⅓ cup packed brown sugar
3 tablespoons MAZOLA® Margarine or butter
¼ cup heavy or whipping cream
1½ cups sliced almonds
1 teaspoon vanilla

1. Preheat oven to 350°F. Prepare Bar Cookie Crust.

2. Meanwhile, in medium saucepan combine corn syrup, brown sugar, margarine and cream. Bring to boil over medium heat; remove from heat. Stir in almonds and vanilla. Spread over hot crust.

3. Bake 12 minutes or until set and golden. Cool completely on wire rack. Cut into 2-inch squares; cut diagonally in half for triangles.

Makes about 48 triangles

Pecan Praline Cookies

PRALINE
- 1½ cups chopped pecans
- ½ cup granulated sugar
- 3 tablespoons water

COOKIES
- 1¼ cups firmly packed light brown sugar
- ¾ BUTTER FLAVOR* CRISCO® Stick
  - or ¾ cup BUTTER FLAVOR CRISCO all-vegetable shortening
- 2 tablespoons milk
- 1 tablespoon vanilla
- 1 egg
- 1¾ cups all-purpose flour
- 1 teaspoon salt
- ¾ teaspoon baking soda

*Butter Flavor Crisco is artificially flavored.

1. Heat oven to 375°F. **Place** sheets of foil on countertop for cooling cookies.

2. *For praline,* **spread** pecans on baking sheet. **Bake** at 375°F for 10 minutes or until lightly toasted, stirring several times. **Reserve** pecans. **Grease** baking sheet.

3. Place granulated sugar and water in small saucepan. **Bring** to boil, stirring occasionally. **Cover;** boil 2 minutes. **Uncover;** cook 2 minutes or until mixture becomes golden brown in color. **Add** reserved pecans; stir until evenly coated. **Spread** on prepared baking sheet. **Cool** completely. **Place** hardened praline in heavy resealable plastic bag; seal. **Crush** with bottom of small heavy skillet until pieces are small.

4. *For cookies,* place brown sugar, shortening, milk and vanilla in large bowl. **Beat** at medium speed of electric mixer until well blended. **Add** egg; beat well.

5. Combine flour, salt and baking soda. **Add** to shortening mixture; beat at low speed just until blended. **Stir** in 1½ cups of crushed praline.

6. Shape dough into 1-inch balls. **Dip** top of each ball into remaining crushed praline. **Place** 3 inches apart on ungreased baking sheets.

7. Bake one baking sheet at a time at 375°F for 9 to 11 minutes or until cookies are lightly browned. *Do not overbake.* **Cool** 2 minutes on baking sheet. **Remove** cookies to foil to cool completely.

Makes about 3 dozen cookies

German Chocolate Brownie Cookies

COOKIES
- 1½ cups firmly packed light brown sugar
- ⅔ CRISCO® Stick or ⅔ cup CRISCO all-vegetable shortening
- 1 tablespoon water
- 1 teaspoon vanilla
- 2 eggs
- 1½ cups all-purpose flour
- ⅓ cup unsweetened cocoa powder
- ½ teaspoon salt
- ¼ teaspoon baking soda
- 2 cups (12 ounces) semisweet chocolate chips

TOPPING
- ½ cup evaporated milk
- ½ cup granulated sugar
- ¼ BUTTER FLAVOR* CRISCO Stick** or ¼ cup BUTTER FLAVOR CRISCO all-vegetable shortening
- 2 egg yolks, lightly beaten
- ½ teaspoon vanilla
- ½ cup chopped pecans
- ½ cup flaked coconut

*Butter Flavor Crisco is artificially flavored.

**Crisco all-vegetable shortening can be substituted for Butter Flavor Crisco Stick or Butter Flavor Crisco.

1. Heat oven to 375°F. **Place** sheets of foil on countertop for cooling cookies.

2. *For cookies*, place brown sugar, shortening, water and vanilla in large bowl. **Beat** at medium speed of electric mixer until well blended. **Add** eggs; beat well.

3. Combine flour, cocoa, salt and baking soda. **Add** to shortening mixture; beat at low speed just until blended. **Stir** in chocolate chips.

4. Drop dough by rounded measuring tablespoonfuls 2 inches apart onto ungreased baking sheet.

5. Bake one baking sheet at a time at 375°F for 7 to 9 minutes or until cookies are set. *Do not overbake.* **Cool** 2 minutes on baking sheet. **Remove** cookies to foil to cool completely.

6. *For topping*, combine evaporated milk, granulated sugar, shortening and egg yolks in medium saucepan. **Stir** over medium heat until thickened. **Remove** from heat. **Stir** in vanilla, pecans and coconut. **Cool** completely. **Frost** cookies.

Makes about 3 dozen cookies

Fudgey German Chocolate Sandwich Cookies

1¾ cups all-purpose flour
1½ cups sugar
¾ cup (1½ sticks) butter or margarine, softened
⅔ cup HERSHEY¡S Cocoa or HERSHEY¡S European Style Cocoa
¾ teaspoon baking soda
¼ teaspoon salt
2 eggs
2 tablespoons milk
1 teaspoon vanilla extract
½ cup finely chopped pecans
Coconut and Pecan Filling (recipe follows)

Heat oven to 350°F. In large bowl, combine flour, sugar, butter, cocoa, baking soda, salt, eggs, milk and vanilla. Beat at medium speed of electric mixer until blended. (Batter will be stiff.) Stir in pecans. Shape dough into 1¼-inch balls. Place on ungreased cookie sheet; flatten slightly. Bake 9 to 11 minutes or until almost set. Cool slightly; remove from cookie sheet to wire rack. Cool completely. Prepare Coconut and Pecan Filling. Spread flat side of one cookie with 1 heaping tablespoon prepared filling; cover with flat side of second cookie. Serve warm or at room temperature.

Makes about 1½ dozen sandwich cookies

Note: Cookies can be reheated in microwave. Microwave at HIGH (100%) 10 seconds, or until filling is warm.

Coconut and Pecan Filling

½ cup (1 stick) butter or margarine
½ cup packed light brown sugar
¼ cup light corn syrup
1 cup MOUNDS® Sweetened Coconut
   Flakes, toasted*
1 cup finely chopped pecans
1 teaspoon vanilla extract

In medium saucepan over medium heat, melt butter.
Add brown sugar and corn syrup; stir constantly until
thick and bubbly. Remove from heat; stir in coconut,
pecans and vanilla. Use warm.

*To toast coconut: Heat oven to 350°F. Spread coconut in even layer
on baking sheet. Bake 6 to 8 minutes or until golden, stirring several
times during toasting.

Mocha Pecan Pinwheels

1   square (1 ounce) unsweetened
      chocolate
½   cup (1 stick) butter or margarine,
      softened
¾   cup packed brown sugar
1   egg
1   teaspoon vanilla extract
¼   teaspoon baking soda
1¾ cups all-purpose flour
½   cup chopped pecans
1   teaspoon instant espresso coffee
      powder

1. Melt chocolate in small bowl over hot, not boiling, water. Stir until smooth; set aside.

2. Beat butter, brown sugar, egg, vanilla and baking soda in large bowl with electric mixer at medium speed, blending well. Stir in flour to make stiff dough. Remove half of dough; place in another bowl. Blend pecans and coffee powder into half of dough. Stir melted chocolate into remaining half of dough. Cover both halves of dough; refrigerate 30 minutes.

3. Roll out light-colored dough to 15×8-inch rectangle between 2 sheets of plastic wrap. Roll chocolate dough out to same dimensions between 2 more sheets of plastic wrap. Remove top sheets of plastic wrap. Place light-colored dough on top of chocolate dough. Remove remaining sheets of plastic wrap. Roll up firmly, jelly-roll fashion, starting with long side. Wrap in plastic; freeze until firm enough to handle. (Dough can be frozen up to 6 weeks.)

4. Preheat oven to 350°F. Line cookie sheets with parchment paper or leave ungreased.

5. Cut frozen dough into ¼-inch-thick slices; place 2 inches apart on prepared cookie sheets. Bake 9 to 12 minutes until set. Remove to wire racks; cool completely. Store tightly covered.

Makes about 5 dozen cookies

Cappuccino Bon Bons

1	package (19.8 ounces) DUNCAN HINES® Chewy Fudge Brownie Mix
2	eggs
⅓	cup water
⅓	cup CRISCO® Oil or CRISCO® PURITAN® Canola Oil
1½	tablespoons FOLGERS® Instant Coffee
1	teaspoon ground cinnamon
	Whipped topping
	Cinnamon

1. Preheat oven to 350°F. Place 2-inch foil cupcake liners on cookie sheet.

2. Combine brownie mix, eggs, water, oil, instant coffee and cinnamon. Stir with spoon until well blended, about 50 strokes. Fill each cupcake liner with 1 measuring tablespoon batter. Bake 12 to 15 minutes or until wooden toothpick inserted in center comes out clean. Cool completely. Garnish with whipped topping and a dash of cinnamon. Refrigerate until ready to serve.

Makes about 40 bon bons

Cappuccino Cookies

1¼ cups firmly packed light brown sugar
1 BUTTER FLAVOR* CRISCO® Stick or
    1 cup BUTTER FLAVOR CRISCO
    all-vegetable shortening
2 eggs
¼ cup light corn syrup or regular pancake
    syrup
1 teaspoon vanilla
1 teaspoon rum extract
2 tablespoons instant espresso or coffee
    powder
3 cups all-purpose flour
¾ teaspoon baking powder
½ teaspoon baking soda
½ teaspoon salt
½ teaspoon nutmeg
    Chocolate jimmies

*Butter Flavor Crisco is artificially flavored.

1. Place brown sugar and shortening in large bowl.
Beat at medium speed of electric mixer until well
blended. **Add** eggs, corn syrup, vanilla, rum extract and
coffee; beat until well blended and fluffy.

2. Combine flour, baking powder, baking soda, salt and
nutmeg. **Add** gradually to shortening mixture, beating
at low speed until blended. **Divide** dough in half. **Roll**
each half into two logs approximately 2 inches in
diameter. **Wrap** in waxed paper. **Refrigerate** several
hours.

3. Heat oven to 350°F. **Place** sheets of foil on countertop for cooling cookies.

4. Cut cookies into ¼-inch-thick slices. **Place** 2 inches apart on ungreased baking sheet. **Sprinkle** center of each cookie with jimmies.

5. Bake one baking sheet at a time at 350°F for 10 to 12 minutes or until golden brown. *Do not overbake.* **Cool** 2 minutes. **Remove** cookies to foil to cool completely.   *Makes about 4½ dozen cookies*

Kentucky Bourbon Pecan Pie Tarts

Cream Cheese Pastry (recipe follows)
3 eggs
1 cup KARO® Dark or Light Corn Syrup
1 cup sugar
¼ cup bourbon
2 tablespoons MAZOLA® Margarine or
    butter, melted
1 teaspoon vanilla
2 cups finely chopped pecans
Confectioners sugar (optional)

1. Prepare Cream Cheese Pastry. On floured surface roll pastry, half at a time, ⅛ inch thick. Cut into 2¼-inch rounds. Press evenly into bottoms and up sides of 1¾×1-inch muffin cups. Refrigerate until ready to use.

2. Preheat oven to 350°F. In medium bowl with fork beat eggs slightly. Stir in corn syrup, sugar, bourbon, margarine and vanilla until blended.

3. Spoon 1 heaping teaspoon pecans into each pastry-lined cup; top with 1 tablespoon corn syrup mixture.

4. Bake 20 to 25 minutes or until lightly browned and cake tester inserted in center comes out clean. Cool in pan 5 minutes. Remove; cool completely on wire racks. Store in tightly covered container. Just before serving, sprinkle with confectioners sugar.

Makes about 5 dozen tarts

Cream Cheese Pastry

1¾ cups flour
1½ teaspoons baking powder
⅛   teaspoon salt
¾   cup (1½ sticks) MAZOLA® Margarine or
      butter
2   packages (3 ounces each) cream
      cheese, softened
1   tablespoon sugar

In small bowl combine flour, baking powder and salt.
In large bowl with mixer at medium speed, beat
margarine, cream cheese and sugar until smooth. Stir
in flour mixture until blended. Press into ball.

Note: Recipe may be halved. For pastry use 1 cup flour
and ½ cup (1 stick) MAZOLA® Margarine. For filling,
use 2 eggs; reduce remaining ingredients by half.

Classic Anise Biscotti

    4 ounces whole blanched almonds (about
       ¾ cup)
 2¼ cups all-purpose flour
    1 teaspoon baking powder
    ¾ teaspoon salt
    ¾ cup sugar
    ½ cup unsalted butter, softened
    3 eggs
    2 tablespoons brandy
    2 teaspoons grated lemon peel
    1 tablespoon whole anise seeds

1. Preheat oven to 375°F. To toast almonds, spread almonds on baking sheet. Bake 6 to 8 minutes until toasted and light brown; turn off oven. Remove almonds with spoon to cutting board; cool. Coarsely chop almonds.

2. Combine flour, baking powder and salt in small bowl. Beat sugar and butter in medium bowl with electric mixer at medium speed until light and fluffy. Add eggs, 1 at a time, beating well after each addition and scraping side of bowl often. Stir in brandy and lemon peel. Add flour mixture gradually; stir until smooth. Stir in almonds and anise seeds. Cover and refrigerate dough 1 hour or until firm.

3. Preheat oven to 375°F. Grease large baking sheet.

4. Divide dough in half. Shape ½ of dough into 12×2-inch log on lightly floured surface. (Dough will be fairly soft.) Pat smooth with lightly floured fingertips. Repeat with remaining ½ of dough to form second log.

5. Bake 20 to 25 minutes until logs are light golden brown. Remove baking sheet from oven to wire rack; turn off oven. Cool logs completely.

6. Preheat oven to 350°F. Cut logs diagonally with serrated knife into ½-inch-thick slices. Place slices flat in single layer on 2 ungreased baking sheets.

7. Bake 8 minutes. Turn slices over; bake 10 to 12 minutes more until cut surfaces are light brown and cookies are dry. Remove cookies to wire racks; cool completely. Store cookies in airtight container up to 2 weeks.   *Makes about 4 dozen cookies*

Chocolate Chip Almond Biscotti

2¾ cups all-purpose flour
1½ teaspoons baking powder
¼ teaspoon salt
½ cup butter or margarine, softened
1 cup sugar
3 eggs
3 tablespoons almond-flavored liqueur
1 tablespoon water
1 cup mini semisweet chocolate chips
1 cup sliced almonds, toasted, chopped

1. Combine flour, baking powder and salt in medium bowl. Beat butter and sugar in large bowl with electric mixer at medium speed until light and fluffy. Beat in eggs, 1 at a time, beating well after each addition. Add liqueur and water. Gradually add flour mixture. Stir in chips and almonds.

2. Divide dough into fourths. Shape each quarter into a 15-inch log. Wrap securely. Refrigerate about 2 hours or until firm.

3. Preheat oven to 375°F. Lightly grease cookie sheet.

4. Place each log on prepared cookie sheet. With floured hands, shape each log 2 inches wide and ½ inch thick.

5. Bake 15 minutes. Remove logs from oven to cutting surface. Cut each log with serrated knife into 1-inch diagonal slices. Return slices, cut sides up, to cookie sheets; bake 7 minutes. Turn cookies over; bake 7 minutes or until cut surfaces are golden brown and cookies are dry. Cool completely. Store tightly covered.

Makes 4 dozen cookies

Chocolate Pistachio Fingers

¾ cup butter or margarine, softened
⅓ cup sugar
⅓ cup (about 3 ounces) almond paste
1 egg yolk
1⅔ cups all-purpose flour
1 cup (6 ounces) semisweet chocolate chips
½ cup finely chopped natural pistachios

1. Preheat oven to 350°F. Line cookie sheets with parchment paper or lightly grease and dust with flour.

2. Beat butter and sugar in large bowl with electric mixer at medium speed until blended. Add almond paste and egg yolk; beat until light. Blend in flour to make a smooth dough. (If dough is too soft to handle, cover and refrigerate until firm.) Turn out onto lightly floured board. Divide dough into 8 equal pieces; divide each piece in half. Roll each half into 12-inch rope; cut each rope into 2-inch lengths. Place 2 inches apart on prepared cookie sheets.

3. Bake 10 to 12 minutes until edges just begin to brown. Remove to wire racks; cool completely.

4. Melt chocolate chips in small bowl over hot water. Stir until smooth. Dip both ends of cookies about ½ inch into melted chocolate, then dip chocolate ends into pistachios. Place on waxed paper; let stand until chocolate is set. Store tightly covered.

Makes 8 dozen cookies

Chocolate Madeleines

3   teaspoons butter, softened, divided
1¼ cups cake flour or all-purpose flour
¼   cup unsweetened cocoa powder
¼   teaspoon salt
¼   teaspoon baking powder
1   cup granulated sugar
2   large eggs
¾   cup butter, melted and cooled
2   tablespoons almond-flavored liqueur or
      kirsch
    Powdered sugar

1. Preheat oven to 375°F. Grease 3 madeleine pans with softened butter, 1 teaspoon per pan; dust with flour. (If only 1 madeleine pan is available, thoroughly wash, dry, regrease and flour after baking each batch. Cover remaining dough with plastic wrap; let stand at room temperature.)

2. Combine flour, cocoa, salt and baking powder in medium bowl. Beat sugar and eggs in large bowl with electric mixer at medium speed 5 minutes or until mixture is light in color, thick and falls in wide ribbons from beaters, scraping down side of bowl once. Beat in flour mixture at low speed until well blended, scraping down side of bowl once. Beat in butter and liqueur until just blended.

3. Spoon level tablespoonfuls of batter into each prepared madeleine mold. Bake 12 minutes or until puffed and golden brown.

4. Let madeleines stand in pan 1 minute. Carefully loosen cookies from pan with point of small knife. Invert pan over wire racks; tap lightly to release cookies. Let stand 2 minutes. Turn cookies shell-sides up; cool completely.

5. Dust with sifted powdered sugar. Store tightly covered at room temperature up to 24 hours or freeze up to 3 months.   *Makes about 2 dozen madeleines*

Almond Rice Madeleines

1   **cup whole blanched almonds, lightly toasted**
¾   **cup flaked coconut**
1½ **cups sugar**
3   **cups cooked rice, chilled**
3   **egg whites**
    Fresh raspberries
    Frozen nondairy whipped topping (optional)

Preheat oven to 350°F. Spray madeleine pans* with nonstick cooking spray. Place almonds in blender or food processor; process until finely ground. Add coconut and sugar to processor; process until coconut is finely minced. Add rice; pulse to blend. Add egg whites; pulse to blend. Spoon mixture evenly into prepared madeleine pans, filling to tops.

Bake 25 to 30 minutes or until lightly browned. Cool completely in pans on wire racks. Cover and refrigerate 2 hours or until ready to serve. Run sharp knife around each shell; gently remove from pan. Invert onto serving plates. Serve with raspberries and whipped topping, if desired.   *Makes about 3 dozen cookies*

*Substitute miniature muffin tins for madeleine pans, if desired.

Favorite recipe from **USA Rice Council**

Chocolate Macaroons

12 ounces semisweet baking chocolate or
chips
1 can (8 ounces) almond paste
2 egg whites
½ cup powdered sugar
2 tablespoons all-purpose flour
Powdered sugar (optional)

1. Preheat oven to 300°F. Line cookie sheets with parchment paper.

2. Melt chocolate in small, heavy saucepan over low heat, stirring constantly; set aside.

3. Beat almond paste, egg whites and sugar in large bowl with electric mixer at medium speed for 1 minute, scraping down side of bowl once. Beat in chocolate until well combined. Beat in flour at low speed, scraping down side of bowl once.

4. Spoon dough into pastry tube fitted with rosette tip. Pipe 1½-inch spirals 1 inch apart onto prepared cookie sheets. Pipe all cookies at once; dough will get stiff upon standing.

5. Bake 20 minutes or until set. Carefully remove parchment paper to countertop; cool completely.

6. Peel cookies off parchment paper. Place powdered sugar in fine-mesh strainer; sprinkle over cookies, if desired. Store tightly covered at room temperature or freeze up to 3 months.

Makes about 3 dozen cookies

🍓 Heavenly 🍓

HOLIDAY TREATS

Cherry Surprises

1 **package DUNCAN HINES® Golden Sugar Cookie Mix**
48 **to 54 candied cherries**
¾ **cup semi-sweet chocolate chips**
1½ **teaspoons CRISCO® all-vegetable shortening**

1. Preheat oven to 375°F. Grease baking sheets.

2. Prepare cookie mix following package directions for cut cookies. Shape thin layer of dough around each candied cherry. Place 2 inches apart on greased baking sheets. Bake at 375°F for 8 minutes or until set but not browned. Cool 1 minute on baking sheets. Remove to cooling racks. Cool completely.

3. Combine chocolate chips and shortening in small resealable plastic bag. Place bag in bowl of hot water for several minutes. Dry with paper towel. Knead until blended and chocolate is smooth. Snip pinpoint corner in bag. Drizzle chocolate over cookies. Allow drizzle to set before storing between layers of waxed paper in airtight containers.   *Makes 4 to 4½ dozen cookies*

Tip: Well-drained maraschino cherries may be substituted for candied cherries.

Almond Cream Cookies

¾ cup (1½ sticks) margarine, softened
¾ cup granulated sugar
½ cup plus 2 tablespoons soft-style cream
     cheese
1 egg
1 teaspoon almond extract
1¼ cups all-purpose flour
¾ cup QUAKER® Corn Meal
½ teaspoon baking powder
½ cup coarsely chopped almonds
1 cup powdered sugar
1 tablespoon milk or water
    Red or green candied cherries

Preheat oven to 350°F. Beat margarine, granulated
sugar and ½ cup cream cheese at medium speed of
electric mixer until light and fluffy. Add egg and
almond extract; mix until well blended. Gradually add
combined flour, corn meal and baking powder; mix
well. Stir in almonds. Drop by rounded teaspoonful
onto ungreased cookie sheets. Bake 12 to 14 minutes
or until edges are golden brown. Cool on cookie sheets
for 2 minutes; remove to wire racks. Cool completely.

Mix remaining 2 tablespoons cream cheese and
powdered sugar until blended. Add milk; mix until
smooth. Spread over cookies. Garnish with halved red
or green candied cherries, if desired. Store tightly
covered.   *Makes about 4 dozen cookies*

Cherry Dot Cookies

2¼ cups all-purpose flour
2 teaspoons baking powder
½ teaspoon salt
¾ cup margarine, softened
1 cup sugar
2 eggs
2 tablespoons skim milk
1 teaspoon vanilla
1 cup chopped nuts
1 cup finely cut pitted dates
⅓ cup finely chopped maraschino cherries
2⅔ cups KELLOGG'S CORN FLAKES®
cereal, crushed to 1⅓ cups
Vegetable cooking spray
15 maraschino cherries, cut into quarters

1. Stir together flour, baking powder and salt. Set aside.

2. In large mixing bowl, beat margarine and sugar until light and fluffy. Add eggs. Beat well. Stir in milk and vanilla. Add flour mixture. Mix well. Stir in nuts, dates and the ⅓ cup chopped cherries.

3. Shape level measuring tablespoons of dough into balls. Roll in KELLOGG'S CORN FLAKES® cereal. Place on baking sheets coated with cooking spray. Top each cookie with cherry quarter.

4. Bake at 350°F about 10 minutes or until lightly browned.   *Makes about 5 dozen cookies*

Chocolate Cherry Cookies

2   squares (1 ounce each) unsweetened
      chocolate
½   cup butter or margarine, softened
½   cup sugar
1   egg
2   cups cake flour
1   teaspoon vanilla extract
¼   teaspoon salt
      Maraschino cherries, well drained
      (about 48)
1   cup (6 ounces) semisweet or milk
      chocolate chips

1. Melt unsweetened chocolate in top of double boiler over hot, not boiling, water. Remove from heat; cool.

2. Beat butter and sugar in large bowl with electric mixer at medium speed until creamy. Add egg and melted chocolate; beat until fluffy. Stir in cake flour, vanilla and salt until well blended. Cover; refrigerate until firm, about 1 hour.

3. Preheat oven to 400°F. Lightly grease cookie sheets or line with parchment paper.

4. Shape dough into 1-inch balls. Place 2 inches apart on prepared cookie sheets. With knuckle of finger, make deep indentation in center of each ball. Place cherry into each indentation.

5. Bake 8 minutes or just until set. Meanwhile, melt chocolate chips in small bowl over hot water. Stir until melted. Remove cookies to wire racks. Drizzle melted chocolate over tops of cookies while still warm. Refrigerate until chocolate is set. Store tightly covered.

Makes about 4 dozen cookies

Chocolate Cherry Drops

- 1　**package DUNCAN HINES® Chocolate Chip Cookie Mix**
- 1　**egg**
- ⅓　**cup CRISCO® Oil or CRISCO® PURITAN® Canola Oil**
- 3　**tablespoons water**
- ⅓　**cup chopped maraschino cherries, well drained**
- ⅓　**cup flaked coconut**
- 2　**cups chopped pecans**

1. Preheat oven to 375°F.

2. Combine cookie mix, egg, oil and water in large bowl. Stir until thoroughly blended. Stir in cherries and coconut. Shape dough into 48 (1-inch) balls. Roll in chopped pecans. Place 2 inches apart on ungreased baking sheets.

3. Bake at 375°F for 11 to 12 minutes or until cookies are set and lightly browned. Cool 1 minute on baking sheets. Remove to cooling racks. Cool completely. Store in airtight containers.

Makes 4 dozen cookies

Chocolate-Cherry
Slice 'n' Bake Cookies

¾ cup (1½ sticks) butter or margarine,
   softened
1 cup sugar
1 egg
1½ teaspoons vanilla extract
2¼ cups all-purpose flour
2 teaspoons baking powder
½ teaspoon salt
¼ cup finely chopped maraschino cherries
½ teaspoon almond extract
   Red food color
⅓ cup HERSHEY'S Cocoa
¼ teaspoon baking soda
4 teaspoons water
   Cocoa Almond Glaze (recipe follows)

In large bowl, beat butter, sugar, egg and vanilla until
light and fluffy. Stir together flour, baking powder and
salt; gradually add to butter mixture, beating until
mixture forms a smooth dough. Remove 1¼ cups
dough to medium bowl; blend in cherries, almond
extract and about 6 drops food color. Stir together
cocoa and baking soda. Add with water to remaining
dough; blend until smooth. Divide chocolate dough in
half; roll each half between two sheets of wax paper,
forming 12×4½-inch rectangle. Remove top sheet of
wax paper from each rectangle. Divide cherry mixture
in half; with floured hands, shape each half into
12-inch roll. Place one roll in center of each rectangle;

wrap chocolate dough around each roll. Wrap each roll in plastic wrap. Refrigerate about 6 hours or until firm. Heat oven to 350°F. Cut rolls into ¼-inch-thick slices; place on ungreased cookie sheet. Bake 7 minutes or until set. Cool 1 minute; remove from cookie sheet to wire rack. Cool completely. Prepare Cocoa Almond Glaze; decorate cookies.

Makes about 7½ dozen cookies

Cocoa Almond Glaze

- 2 **tablespoons butter or margarine**
- 2 **tablespoons HERSHEY'S Cocoa**
- 2 **tablespoons water**
- 1 **cup powdered sugar**
- ⅛ **teaspoon almond extract**

In small saucepan over low heat, melt butter. Add cocoa and water; stir constantly until mixture thickens. *Do not boil.* Remove from heat. Add sugar and almond extract, beating until smooth and of desired consistency.

Jam Thumbprint Gems

1½ cups all-purpose flour
1 teaspoon baking powder
½ teaspoon salt
½ teaspoon ground cinnamon
¼ teaspoon ground cloves
¼ cup MOTT'S® Natural Apple Sauce
2 tablespoons vegetable shortening
½ cup plus 1 tablespoon powdered sugar, divided
1 egg
½ teaspoon vanilla extract
½ cup strawberry or other favorite flavor preserves

1. Preheat oven to 400°F. Spray cookie sheet with nonstick cooking spray.

2. In small bowl, combine flour, baking powder, salt and spices.

3. In large bowl, whisk together apple sauce and shortening until shortening breaks into pea-sized pieces. Add ½ cup powdered sugar; stir well. Add egg and vanilla; mix well.

4. Add flour mixture to apple sauce mixture; stir until well blended. (Mixture will be stiff.)

5. Using flour-coated hands, roll teaspoonfuls of dough into balls. Place 1 inch apart on prepared cookie sheet. Press thumb gently into center of each ball. Spoon ½ teaspoon preserves into each indentation.

6. Bake 12 to 15 minutes or until lightly browned.
Cool completely on wire rack; sprinkle with remaining
1 tablespoon powdered sugar.

Makes 2 dozen cookies

Santa's Thumbprints

    1   cup (2 sticks) margarine, softened
    ½   cup firmly packed brown sugar
    1   whole egg or egg white
    1   teaspoon vanilla
    1½ cups QUAKER® Oats (Quick or Old
          Fashioned), uncooked
    1½ cups all-purpose flour
    1   cup finely chopped nuts
    ⅓   cup jelly or preserves

Heat oven to 350°F. Beat margarine and sugar in large
bowl until light and fluffy. Blend in egg and vanilla. In
large bowl, combine oats and flour; add to margarine
mixture. Mix well. Shape into 1-inch balls; roll in
chopped nuts. Place 2 inches apart on ungreased
cookie sheet. Make indentation in center of each ball
with thumb. Fill each thumbprint with about ¼
teaspoon jelly. Bake 12 to 15 minutes or until light
golden brown. Cool completely on wire rack. Store
loosely covered.   *Makes about 3 dozen cookies*

Double Almond Butter Cookies

DOUGH
- 2 cups butter, softened
- 2½ cups powdered sugar, divided
- 4 cups all-purpose flour
- 2 teaspoons vanilla

FILLING
- ⅔ cup BLUE DIAMOND® Blanched Almond Paste
- ¼ cup packed light brown sugar
- ½ cup BLUE DIAMOND® Chopped Natural Almonds, toasted
- ¼ teaspoon vanilla

For Dough, beat butter and 1 cup powdered sugar. Gradually beat in flour. Beat in 2 teaspoons vanilla. Chill dough ½ hour.

For Filling, combine almond paste, brown sugar, almonds and ¼ teaspoon vanilla.

Preheat oven to 350°F. Shape dough around ½ teaspoon Filling mixture to form 1-inch balls. Place on ungreased cookie sheets.

Bake 15 minutes. Cool on wire racks. Roll cookies in remaining 1½ cups powdered sugar or sift over cookies.

Makes about 8 dozen cookies

European Kolacky

1   cup butter or margarine, softened
1   package (8 ounces) cream cheese,
      softened
1   tablespoon milk
1   tablespoon sugar
1   egg yolk
1½ cups all-purpose flour
½   teaspoon baking powder
1   can SOLO® or 1 jar BAKER® Filling
      (any flavor)
    Confectioners' sugar

Beat butter, cream cheese, milk and sugar in medium
bowl with electric mixer until thoroughly blended.
Beat in egg yolk. Sift together flour and baking
powder; stir into butter mixture to make stiff dough.
Cover and refrigerate several hours or overnight.

Preheat oven to 400°F. Roll out dough on lightly
floured surface to ¼-inch thickness. Cut dough with
floured 2-inch cookie cutter. Place cookies on
ungreased cookie sheets about 1 inch apart. Make
depression in centers of cookies with thumb or back of
spoon. Spoon 1 teaspoon filling into centers of cookies.

Bake 10 to 12 minutes or until lightly browned.
Remove from baking sheets and cool completely on
wire racks. Sprinkle with confectioners' sugar just
before serving.   *Makes about 3 dozen cookies*

Kolacky

½ **cup butter or margarine, softened**
3 **ounces cream cheese, softened**
1 **teaspoon vanilla extract**
1 **cup all-purpose flour**
⅛ **teaspoon salt**
6 **teaspoons fruit preserves (any flavor)**
1 **egg**
1 **teaspoon cold water**
   Powdered sugar (optional)

1. Beat butter and cream cheese in large bowl with electric mixer at medium speed until smooth and creamy. Blend in vanilla. Combine flour and salt; gradually add to butter mixture, mixing until mixture forms soft dough. Divide dough in half; wrap each half in plastic wrap. Refrigerate until firm.

2. Preheat oven to 375°F.

3. Roll out half of dough on lightly floured pastry cloth or board to ⅛-inch thickness. Cut with top of glass or biscuit cutter into 3-inch rounds. Spoon ½ teaspoon preserves onto center of each dough circle. Beat egg with water; lightly brush onto edges of dough circles. Bring 3 edges of dough up over fruit spread; pinch edges together to seal. Place on ungreased cookie sheets; brush with egg mixture. Repeat with remaining dough, fruit spread and egg mixture.

4. Bake 12 minutes or until golden brown. Let stand on cookie sheets 1 minute; transfer to wire racks. Cool completely. Sprinkle with powdered sugar, if desired. Store tightly covered.   *Makes 2 dozen cookies*

Norwegian Wreaths (Berliner Kranser)

1 **hard-cooked large egg yolk**
1 **large egg, separated**
½ **cup butter, softened**
½ **cup powdered sugar**
½ **teaspoon vanilla extract**
1¼ **cups all-purpose flour**
   Coarse sugar crystals or crushed sugar cubes

1. Preheat oven to 350°F. Grease cookie sheets.

2. Beat cooked and raw egg yolks in medium bowl with electric mixer at medium speed until smooth. Beat in butter, powdered sugar and vanilla, scraping down side of bowl once. Stir in 1 cup flour with spoon. Stir in additional flour until stiff dough forms.

3. Place dough on sheet of waxed paper. Using waxed paper to hold dough, roll it back and forth to form a log; cut into 18 equal pieces. Roll each piece of dough into an 8-inch rope, tapering ends.

4. Shape ropes into wreaths; overlap ends and let extend out from wreath. Place wreaths on prepared cookie sheets. Refrigerate 15 minutes or until firm.

5. Beat reserved egg white with fork until foamy. Brush wreaths with egg white; sprinkle with sugar crystals. Bake 8 to 10 minutes until light golden brown. Remove cookies with spatula to wire racks; cool completely. Store tightly covered at room temperature or freeze up to 3 months.

Makes about 1½ dozen cookies

Jammy Pinwheels

1¼ cups granulated sugar
1 BUTTER FLAVOR* CRISCO® Stick or
   1 cup BUTTER FLAVOR CRISCO
   all-vegetable shortening
2 eggs
¼ cup light corn syrup or regular pancake
   syrup
1 tablespoon vanilla
3 cups all-purpose flour (plus
   2 tablespoons), divided
¾ teaspoon baking powder
½ teaspoon baking soda
½ teaspoon salt
1 cup apricot, strawberry or seedless
   raspberry jam

*Butter Flavor Crisco is artificially flavored.

1. Place sugar and shortening in large bowl. **Beat** at medium speed of electric mixer until well blended. **Add** eggs, syrup and vanilla; beat until well blended and fluffy.

2. Combine 3 cups flour, baking powder, baking soda and salt. **Add** gradually to shortening mixture, beating at low speed until well blended.

3. Divide dough in half. **Pat** each half into thick rectangle. **Sprinkle** about 1 tablespoon flour on large sheet of waxed paper. **Place** rectangle of dough on floured paper. **Turn** dough over; cover with another large sheet of waxed paper. **Roll** dough into an 8×12-inch rectangle about ⅛ inch thick. **Trim** edges. **Slide** dough and waxed paper onto ungreased baking sheets. **Refrigerate** 20 minutes or until firm. **Repeat** with remaining dough.

4. Heat oven to 375°F. **Grease** baking sheets. **Place** sheets of foil on counter for cooling cookies.

5. Place chilled dough rectangle on work surface. **Remove** top sheet of waxed paper. **Cut** dough into 2-inch squares. **Place** squares 2 inches apart on prepared baking sheets. **Make** a 1-inch diagonal cut from each corner of square almost to center. **Place** 1 teaspoon jam in center. **Lift** every other corner and bring together in center of cookie. **Repeat** with remaining dough.

6. Bake at 375°F for 7 to 10 minutes or until edges of cookies are golden brown. *Do not overbake.* **Cool** 2 minutes on baking sheet. **Remove** cookies to foil to cool completely.   *Makes about 4 dozen cookies*

Lemon Pecan Crescents

1   **package DUNCAN HINES® Golden Sugar Cookie Mix**
2   **egg whites**
¾   **cup toasted pecans, chopped**
⅓   **cup CRISCO® Oil or CRISCO® PURITAN® Canola Oil**
¼   **cup all-purpose flour**
1   **tablespoon grated lemon peel**
    Confectioners sugar

1. Preheat oven to 375°F.

2. Combine cookie mix, egg whites, pecans, oil, flour and lemon peel in large bowl. Stir until thoroughly blended. Form level ½ measuring tablespoonfuls dough into crescent shapes. Place 2 inches apart on ungreased baking sheets.

3. Bake 7 to 8 minutes or until set but not browned. Cool 2 minutes. Remove to cooling racks. Roll warm cookies in confectioners sugar. Cool completely. Roll cookies again in confectioners sugar. Store between layers of waxed paper in airtight container.

Makes about 6 dozen cookies

Cocoa Pecan Crescents

1 cup (2 sticks) butter or margarine,
   softened
⅔ cup granulated sugar
1½ teaspoons vanilla extract
1¾ cups all-purpose flour
⅓ cup HERSHEY®'S Cocoa
⅛ teaspoon salt
1½ cups ground pecans
   Powdered sugar

In large bowl, beat butter, granulated sugar and vanilla
until light and fluffy. Stir together flour, cocoa and salt;
gradually add to butter mixture, blending well. Stir in
pecans. Cover; refrigerate dough about 1 hour or until
firm. Heat oven to 375°F. Shape scant tablespoonfuls of
dough into logs about 2½ inches long; place on
ungreased cookie sheet. Shape logs into crescents,
tapering ends. Bake 13 to 15 minutes or until set. Cool
slightly; remove from cookie sheet to wire rack. Cool
completely. Roll in powdered sugar.

Makes about 3½ dozen cookies

Walnut Crescents

3¾ cups flour
½ teaspoon cinnamon
1½ cups (3 sticks) MAZOLA® Margarine or
      butter
¾ cup KARO® Light or Dark
      Corn Syrup
1 tablespoon vanilla
2¼ cups ground walnuts
1½ cups confectioners sugar

1. In medium bowl combine flour and cinnamon; set aside.

2. In large bowl with mixer at medium speed, beat margarine until creamy. Gradually beat in corn syrup and vanilla until well blended. Stir in flour mixture and walnuts.

3. Cover; refrigerate several hours or until easy to handle.

4. Preheat oven to 350°F. Shape rounded teaspoonfuls of dough into 2-inch-long rolls. Place 2 inches apart on ungreased cookie sheets, curving to form crescents.

5. Bake 15 to 18 minutes or until bottoms are lightly browned. Remove from cookie sheets; cool completely on wire racks. Roll in confectioners sugar.

Makes about 8 dozen cookies

Snow-Covered Almond Crescents

- 1 cup (2 sticks) margarine or butter, softened
- ¾ cup powdered sugar
- ½ teaspoon almond extract *or* 2 teaspoons vanilla
- 1¾ cups all-purpose flour
- ¼ teaspoon salt (optional)
- 1 cup QUAKER® Oats (quick or old fashioned, uncooked)
- ½ cup finely chopped almonds
  Powdered sugar

Preheat oven to 325°F. Beat margarine, sugar and almond extract until fluffy. Add flour and salt; mix until well blended. Stir in oats and almonds. Using level measuring tablespoonfuls, shape dough into crescents. Bake on ungreased cookie sheet 14 to 17 minutes or until bottoms are light golden brown. Remove to wire rack. Sift additional powdered sugar generously over warm cookies. Cool completely. Store tightly covered.   *Makes about 3 dozen cookies*

Snowballs

- ½ cup DOMINO® Confectioners 10-X Sugar
- ¼ teaspoon salt
- 1 cup butter or margarine, softened
- 1 teaspoon vanilla extract
- 2¼ cups all-purpose flour
- ½ cup chopped pecans
  Additional DOMINO® Confectioners 10-X Sugar

In large bowl, combine ½ cup sugar, salt and butter; mix well. Add vanilla. Gradually stir in flour. Mix nuts into dough. Cover and chill until firm.

Preheat oven to 400°F. Form dough into 1-inch balls. Place 1 inch apart on ungreased cookie sheets. Bake 8 to 10 minutes or until set, but not brown. Roll in additional sugar immediately. Cool on wire racks. Roll in sugar again. Store in airtight container.

Makes about 5 dozen cookies

Cocoa Kiss Cookies

1   cup (2 sticks) butter or margarine,
     softened
⅔   cup granulated sugar
1   teaspoon vanilla extract
1⅔ cups all-purpose flour
¼   cup HERSHEY'S Cocoa
1   cup finely chopped pecans
1   bag (9 ounces) HERSHEY'S KISSES®
     Milk Chocolates
     Powdered sugar

In large bowl, beat butter, granulated sugar and vanilla
until creamy. Stir together flour and cocoa; gradually
add to butter mixture, beating until blended. Add
pecans; beat until well blended. Refrigerate dough
about 1 hour or until firm enough to handle. Heat
oven to 375°F. Remove wrappers from chocolate pieces.
Mold scant tablespoon of dough around each chocolate
piece, covering completely. Shape into balls. Place on
ungreased cookie sheet. Bake 10 to 12 minutes or until
set. Cool slightly, about 1 minute; remove from cookie
sheet to wire rack. Cool completely. Roll in powdered
sugar. Roll in powdered sugar again just before serving,
if desired.   *Makes about 4½ dozen cookies*

Dusted Cocoa-Cinnamon Cookies

1 cup (2 sticks) butter or margarine, softened
⅔ cup granulated sugar
2 teaspoons milk
2 teaspoons vanilla extract
1⅔ cups all-purpose flour
⅓ cup HERSHEY₀S Cocoa
1 cup finely chopped toasted almonds*
1 cup powdered sugar
1 tablespoon ground cinnamon

In large bowl, beat butter and granulated sugar until creamy. Add milk and vanilla; beat well. Stir together flour and cocoa; gradually add to butter mixture, beating until well blended. Stir in almonds. Cover; refrigerate dough 1 hour or until firm enough to handle. Heat oven to 350°F. Shape dough into finger shapes, each 3 inches long and ½ inch wide. Place on ungreased cookie sheet. Bake 20 minutes or until set; remove from cookie sheet to wire rack. Cool slightly. In small bowl, stir together powdered sugar and cinnamon. Roll warm cookies in powdered sugar mixture. Cool completely.

Makes about 3½ dozen cookies

*To toast almonds: Heat oven to 350°F. Spread almonds in even layer in shallow baking pan. Bake 8 to 10 minutes or until light golden brown, stirring occasionally; cool.

Walnut Christmas Balls

1 **cup California walnuts**
⅔ **cup powdered sugar, divided**
1 **cup butter or margarine, softened**
1 **teaspoon vanilla**
1¾ **cups all-purpose flour**
Chocolate Filling (recipe follows)

Preheat oven to 350°F. In food processor or blender, process walnuts with 2 tablespoons of the sugar until finely ground; set aside. In large bowl, beat butter and remaining sugar. Beat in vanilla. Add flour and ¾ cup of the ground walnuts; mix until blended. Roll dough into about 3 dozen walnut-size balls. Place 2 inches apart on ungreased cookie sheets.

Bake 10 to 12 minutes or until just golden around edges. Remove to wire racks to cool completely.

Prepare Chocolate Filling. Place generous teaspoonful of filling on flat side of half of the cookies. Top with remaining cookies, flat sides down, forming sandwiches. Roll chocolate edges in remaining walnuts.
Makes about 1½ dozen sandwich cookies

Chocolate Filling: Chop 3 squares (1 ounce each) semisweet chocolate; place in food processor or blender with ½ teaspoon vanilla. In saucepan, heat 2 tablespoons *each* butter or margarine and whipping cream over medium heat until hot; add to chocolate. Process until melted, turning machine off and scraping side as needed. With machine on, gradually add 1 cup powdered sugar; process until smooth.

Favorite recipe from **Walnut Marketing Board**

Cinnamon Nut Chocolate Spirals

1½ cups all-purpose flour
¼ teaspoon salt
⅓ cup butter or margarine, softened
¾ cup sugar, divided
1 large egg
1 cup mini semisweet chocolate chips
1 cup very finely chopped walnuts
2 teaspoons ground cinnamon
3 tablespoons butter or margarine, melted

1. Combine flour and salt in small bowl. Beat softened butter and ½ cup sugar in large bowl with electric mixer at medium speed until light and fluffy, scraping down side of bowl once. Beat in egg. Gradually add flour mixture, mixing with mixing spoon. Dough will be stiff. (If necessary, knead dough by hand until it holds together.)

2. Roll out dough between 2 sheets of waxed paper into 12×10-inch rectangle. Remove waxed paper from top of rectangle.

3. Combine chips, walnuts, remaining ¼ cup sugar and cinnamon in medium bowl. Pour hot melted butter over mixture; mix well. (Chocolate will partially melt.) Spoon mixture over dough. Spread evenly with small spatula, leaving ½-inch border on long edges.

4. Using bottom sheet of waxed paper as a guide and starting at long side, tightly roll up dough jelly-roll fashion, removing waxed paper as you roll. Wrap in plastic wrap; refrigerate 30 minutes to 1 hour.*

5. Preheat oven to 350°F. Lightly grease cookie sheets.

6. Unwrap dough. Using heavy thread or dental floss, cut dough into ½-inch slices. Place slices 2 inches apart on prepared cookie sheets.

7. Bake 14 minutes or until edges are light golden brown. Remove cookies with spatula to wire racks; cool completely. Store tightly covered at room temperature or freeze up to 3 months.

Makes about 2 dozen cookies

*If dough is chilled longer than 1 hour, slice with a sharp, thin knife.

Festive Chocolate Chip Drops

4   milk chocolate candy bars (1.55 ounces
     each)
1   package DUNCAN HINES® Chocolate
     Chip Cookie Mix
1   egg
⅓   cup CRISCO® Oil or CRISCO®
     PURITAN® Canola Oil
3   tablespoons water
48 miniature candy canes
     Nonpareils (optional)

1. Preheat oven to 375°F.

2. Separate each candy bar along scored lines into 12
sections.

3. Combine cookie mix, egg, oil and water in large
bowl. Stir until thoroughly blended. Drop by rounded
teaspoonfuls 2 inches apart onto ungreased baking
sheets.

4. Bake at 375°F for 8 to 10 minutes or until light
golden brown. Immediately place 1 chocolate candy
section in center of each cookie. Cool 1 minute on
baking sheets. Remove to cooling racks. Cool slightly.
Lay candy cane on each melted chocolate section, or
spread melted chocolate slightly and sprinkle with
nonpareils, if desired. Cool completely. Store in
airtight containers.   *Makes 4 dozen cookies*

Tip: In place of candy canes, crush peppermint candies
and sprinkle on top of chocolate.

Holiday Fruit Drops

½ cup butter, softened
¾ cup packed brown sugar
1 egg
1¼ cups all-purpose flour
1 teaspoon vanilla extract
½ teaspoon baking soda
½ teaspoon ground cinnamon
   Pinch salt
1 cup (8 ounces) diced candied pineapple
1 cup (8 ounces) red and green whole
      candied cherries
8 ounces chopped pitted dates
1 cup semisweet chocolate chips
½ cup whole hazelnuts
½ cup pecan halves
½ cup coarsely chopped walnuts

1. Preheat oven to 325°F. Lightly grease cookie sheets
or line with parchment paper.

2. Beat butter and sugar in large bowl with electric
mixer at medium speed until creamy. Beat in egg until
light and fluffy. Mix in flour, vanilla, baking soda,
cinnamon and salt. Stir in pineapple, cherries, dates,
chocolate chips, hazelnuts, pecans and walnuts. Drop
dough by rounded teaspoonfuls 2 inches apart onto
prepared cookie sheets.

3. Bake 15 to 20 minutes until firm and lightly
browned around edges. Remove to wire racks; cool
completely. Store tightly covered.

Makes about 8 dozen cookies

Pistachio and White Chocolate Cookies

1   **cup shelled pistachio nuts**
1¼ **cups firmly packed light brown sugar**
¾   **BUTTER FLAVOR* CRISCO® Stick or**
    ¾ cup BUTTER FLAVOR CRISCO
    all-vegetable shortening
2   **tablespoons milk**
1   **tablespoon vanilla**
1   **egg**
1¾ **cups all-purpose flour**
1   **teaspoon salt**
¾   **teaspoon baking soda**
1   **cup white chocolate chips or chunks**

*Butter Flavor Crisco is artificially flavored.

1. Heat oven to 350°F. **Spread** pistachio nuts on baking sheet. **Bake** at 350°F for 7 to 10 minutes or until toasted, stirring several times. **Place** nuts in kitchen towel; rub with towel to remove most of skin. **Cool** nuts. **Chop** coarsely; reserve.

2. *Increase oven temperature to 375°F.* **Place** sheets of foil on countertop for cooling cookies.

3. Place brown sugar, shortening, milk and vanilla in large bowl. **Beat** at medium speed of electric mixer until well blended. **Add** egg; beat well.

4. Combine flour, salt and baking soda. **Add** to shortening mixture; beat at low speed just until blended. **Stir** in white chocolate chips and reserved pistachios.

5. Drop dough by rounded measuring tablespoonfuls 3 inches apart onto ungreased baking sheets.

6. Bake one baking sheet at a time at 375°F for 8 to 10 minutes for chewy cookies, or 11 to 13 minutes for crisp cookies. *Do not overbake.* **Cool** 2 minutes on baking sheet. **Remove** cookies to foil to cool completely. *Makes about 3 dozen cookies*

Frosty's Colorful Cookies

1¼ cups firmly packed light brown sugar
¾ BUTTER FLAVOR* CRISCO® Stick or
   ¾ cup BUTTER FLAVOR CRISCO
   all-vegetable shortening
2 tablespoons milk
1 tablespoon vanilla
1 egg
1¾ cups all-purpose flour
1 teaspoon salt
¾ teaspoon baking soda
2 cups red and green candy-coated
   chocolate pieces

1. Heat oven to 375°F. **Place** sheets of foil on countertop for cooling cookies.

2. Place brown sugar, shortening, milk and vanilla in large bowl. **Beat** at medium speed of electric mixer until well blended. **Add** egg; beat well.

3. Combine flour, salt and baking soda. **Add** to shortening mixture; beat at low speed just until blended. **Stir** in candy-coated chocolate pieces.

4. Drop dough by rounded measuring tablespoonfuls 3 inches apart onto ungreased baking sheets.

5. Bake one baking sheet at a time at 375°F for 8 to 10 minutes for chewy cookies, or 11 to 13 minutes for crisp cookies. *Do not overbake.* **Cool** 2 minutes on baking sheet. **Remove** cookies to foil to cool completely.   *Makes about 3 dozen cookies*

*Butter Flavor Crisco is artificially flavored.

Maple Walnut Cookies

1¼ cups firmly packed light brown sugar
¾ BUTTER FLAVOR* CRISCO® Stick or
   ¾ cup BUTTER FLAVOR CRISCO
   all-vegetable shortening
2 tablespoons maple syrup
1 teaspoon vanilla
1 teaspoon maple extract
1 egg
1¾ cups all-purpose flour
1 teaspoon salt
¾ teaspoon baking soda
½ teaspoon cinnamon
1½ cups chopped walnuts
30 to 40 walnut halves

1. Heat oven to 375°F. **Place** sheets of foil on countertop for cooling cookies.

2. Place brown sugar, shortening, maple syrup, vanilla and maple extract in large bowl. **Beat** at medium speed of electric mixer until well blended. **Add** egg; beat well.

3. Combine flour, salt, baking soda and cinnamon. **Add** to shortening mixture; beat at low speed just to blend. **Stir** in chopped walnuts. **Drop** by rounded measuring tablespoonfuls 3 inches apart onto ungreased baking sheets. **Press** walnut half into center of each cookie.

4. Bake one baking sheet at a time at 375°F for 8 to 10 minutes for chewy cookies, or 11 to 13 minutes for crisp cookies. *Do not overbake.* **Cool** 2 minutes on baking sheet. **Remove** cookies to foil to cool completely.   *Makes about 3 dozen cookies*

*Butter Flavor Crisco is artificially flavored.

Doubly Chocolate Mint Cookies

1 HERSHEY₅S Cookies 'n' Mint Milk
   Chocolate Bar (7 ounces)
½ cup (1 stick) butter or margarine,
   softened
¾ cup sugar
1 egg
1 teaspoon vanilla extract
1 cup all-purpose flour
⅓ cup HERSHEY₅S Cocoa
½ teaspoon baking soda
⅛ teaspoon salt
1 cup coarsely chopped nuts (optional)

Heat oven to 350°F. Cut chocolate bar into small
pieces. In large bowl, beat butter, sugar, egg and vanilla
until light and fluffy. Stir together flour, cocoa, baking
soda and salt; add butter mixture, beating until well
blended. Stir in chocolate pieces and nuts, if desired.
Drop dough by rounded teaspoonfuls onto ungreased
cookie sheet. Bake 10 to 12 minutes or until set. Cool
slightly; remove from cookie sheet to wire rack. Cool
completely.   *Makes about 2½ dozen cookies*

Raspberry Meringue Bars

1 cup butter or margarine, softened
½ cup firmly packed brown sugar
1 egg
2 cups all-purpose flour
1 can SOLO® or 1 jar BAKER® Raspberry
    Filling
MERINGUE TOPPING
3 egg whites
¾ cup granulated sugar
½ cup shredded coconut
½ cup slivered almonds

Preheat oven to 325°F. Grease 13×9-inch baking pan.
Beat butter and brown sugar in medium bowl with
electric mixer at medium speed until light and fluffy.
Add 1 egg; beat until blended. Stir in flour until well
combined. Pat dough evenly in prepared pan. Bake 20
minutes. Remove from oven; spread raspberry filling
over crust. (Do not turn oven off.)

For Meringue Topping, beat egg whites in medium
bowl with electric mixer at high speed until soft peaks
form. Add granulated sugar gradually; beat until stiff
and glossy. Fold coconut and almonds into beaten egg
white mixture. Spread over raspberry filling. Return to
oven. Bake 20 minutes or until Meringue Topping is
lightly browned. Cool completely in pan on wire rack.
Cut into 48 bars. *Makes 48 bars*

Date-Nut Macaroons

1 **(8-ounce) package pitted dates, chopped**
1½ **cups flaked coconut**
1 **cup PLANTERS® Pecan Halves,**
   chopped
¾ **cup sweetened condensed milk (not**
   evaporated milk)
½ **teaspoon vanilla**

Preheat oven to 350°F.

In medium bowl, combine dates, coconut and nuts; blend in sweetened condensed milk and vanilla. Drop by rounded tablespoonfuls onto greased and floured cookie sheets. Bake for 10 to 12 minutes or until light golden brown. Carefully remove from cookie sheets; cool completely on wire racks. Store in airtight container.   *Makes about 2 dozen cookies*

Old World Pfeffernüsse Cookies

½   cup butter or margarine, softened
¾   cup packed brown sugar
½   cup molasses
1   egg
1   tablespoon licorice-flavored liqueur
       (optional)
3¼ cups all-purpose flour
1   teaspoon baking soda
1   teaspoon ground cinnamon
½   teaspoon ground cloves
¼   teaspoon ground nutmeg
      Dash pepper
      Powdered sugar

1. Preheat oven to 350°F. Grease cookie sheets.

2. Beat butter and brown sugar in large bowl with electric mixer at medium speed until creamy. Beat in molasses, egg and liqueur, if desired, until light and fluffy. Mix in flour, baking soda, cinnamon, cloves, nutmeg and pepper. Shape level tablespoonfuls of dough into balls. Place 2 inches apart onto prepared cookie sheets.

3. Bake 12 to 14 minutes until set. Cool 2 minutes on cookie sheets. Remove to wire racks; sprinkle with powdered sugar. Cool completely. Store tightly covered.   *Makes about 4 dozen cookies*

Two-Toned Spritz Cookies

1   **square (1 ounce) unsweetened**
     chocolate, coarsely chopped
1   **cup butter or margarine, softened**
1   **cup sugar**
1   **egg**
1   **teaspoon vanilla extract**
2¼ **cups all-purpose flour**
¼   **teaspoon salt**

1. Melt chocolate in small, heavy saucepan over low heat, stirring constantly; set aside.

2. Beat butter and sugar in large bowl with electric mixer at medium speed until light and fluffy. Beat in egg and vanilla. Combine flour and salt in medium bowl; gradually add to butter mixture. Reserve 2 cups dough. Beat chocolate into dough in bowl until smooth. Cover both doughs and refrigerate about 20 minutes or until firm enough to handle.

3. Preheat oven to 400°F.

4. Roll out vanilla dough between two sheets of waxed paper to ½-inch thickness. Cut into 5×4-inch rectangles. Place chocolate dough on sheet of waxed paper. Roll dough back and forth to form a log 1 inch in diameter. Cut into 5-inch-long logs. Place chocolate log in center of vanilla rectangle. Wrap vanilla dough around log; fit into cookie press with star disc. Press dough onto ungreased cookie sheets 1½ inches apart.

5. Bake about 10 minutes or until just set. Cool cookies on wire racks. Store tightly covered.

Makes about 4 dozen cookies

Spritz Christmas Trees

⅓ cup (3½ ounces) almond paste
1 egg
¼ cup CRISCO® Oil or CRISCO®
   PURITAN® Canola Oil
1 tablespoon water
8 drops green food coloring
1 package DUNCAN HINES® Golden
   Sugar Cookie Mix
1 container DUNCAN HINES® Creamy
   Homestyle Vanilla Frosting
   Cinnamon candies, for garnish

1. Preheat oven to 375°F. Combine almond paste and egg in large bowl. Beat at low speed with electric mixer until blended. Add oil, water and green food coloring. Beat until smooth and evenly tinted. Add cookie mix. Beat at low speed until thoroughly blended.

2. Fit cookie press with Christmas tree plate; fill with dough. Force dough through press, 2 inches apart, onto ungreased baking sheets. Bake at 375°F for 6 to 7 minutes or until set but not browned. Cool 1 minute. Remove to cooling racks. Cool completely.

3. To decorate, fill resealable plastic bag half full with Vanilla frosting. Do not seal bag. Cut pinpoint hole in bottom corner of bag. Pipe small dot of frosting onto tip of one cookie tree and top with cinnamon candy. Repeat with remaining cookies. Pipe remaining frosting to form garland on cookie trees. Allow frosting to set before storing between layers of waxed paper in airtight container. *Makes about 6 dozen cookies*

Christmas Ornament Cookies

2¼ cups all-purpose flour
¼ teaspoon salt
1 cup granulated sugar
¾ cup butter or margarine, softened
1 large egg
1 teaspoon vanilla extract
1 teaspoon almond extract
   Icing (recipe follows)
   Assorted food coloring
   Assorted candies or decors

1. Combine flour and salt in medium bowl. Beat sugar and butter in large bowl with electric mixer at medium speed until light and fluffy, scraping down side of bowl once. Beat in egg, vanilla and almond extract. Gradually add flour mixture. Beat at low speed until well blended, scraping down side of bowl once.

2. Form dough into 2 discs; wrap in plastic wrap and refrigerate 30 minutes or until firm.

3. Preheat oven to 350°F.

4. Working with 1 disc at a time, unwrap dough and place on lightly floured surface. Roll out dough with lightly floured rolling pin to ¼-inch thickness. Cut dough into desired shapes with assorted floured cookie cutters. Place cutouts on ungreased cookie sheets. Using drinking straw or tip of sharp knife, cut a hole near top of cookie to allow for piece of ribbon or string to be inserted for hanger. Gently press dough trimmings together; reroll and cut out more cookies.

5. Bake 10 to 12 minutes until edges are golden brown. Let cookies stand on cookie sheets 1 minute. Remove cookies with spatula to wire racks; cool completely.

6. Prepare Icing. Spoon white Icing into small resealable plastic food storage bag. Cut off very tiny corner of bag; pipe Icing decoratively over cookies. Decorate with additional Icing colors and candies as desired. Let stand at room temperature 40 minutes or until set. Thread ribbon through cookie hole to hang as Christmas tree ornament.

Makes about 2 dozen cookies

Icing

2   **cups powdered sugar**
2   **tablespoons milk or lemon juice**

Place powdered sugar and milk in small bowl; stir with spoon until smooth. (Icing will be very thick. If it is too thick, stir in 1 teaspoon additional milk.) If desired, Icing may be divided into small bowls and tinted with food coloring.

Christmas Stained Glass Cookies

        Hard candies (in assorted colors)
 ¾ **cup butter, softened**
 ¾ **cup white granulated sugar**
 2 **eggs**
 1 **teaspoon vanilla extract**
 3 **cups all-purpose flour**
 1 **teaspoon baking powder**
        Frosting (optional)
        Candy (optional)

Separate colors of hard candy. Place each color of candy in small freezer-weight plastic food storage bag; crush with a wooden mallet.* In large mixing bowl, beat together butter and sugar. Beat in eggs and vanilla. Combine flour and baking powder in medium bowl. Gradually stir into butter mixture until dough is very stiff. Wrap in plastic wrap; refrigerate about 3 hours or until firm.

Preheat oven to 375°F. Roll out dough to ⅛-inch thickness on lightly floured surface. Additional flour can be added, if necessary. Cut out cookies using large Christmas cookie cutters. Transfer cookies to foil-lined baking sheet. Using small Christmas cookie cutter of the same shape as the large one, cut out and remove dough from center of each cookie.** Fill cutout sections with crushed candy. If using cookies as hanging ornaments, make holes with a straw at top of cookies for string.

*You will need a total measurement of ⅛ cup crushed.

**Other shapes can be used to cut out center to make different designs.

Bake 7 to 9 minutes or until cookies are lightly browned and candy is melted. Slide foil off baking sheets. When cool, carefully loosen cookies from foil. If desired, decorate with frosting and other candies.

Makes about 2½ dozen cookies

Favorite recipe from **The Sugar Association, Inc.**

Ultimate Sugar Cookies

1¼ cups granulated sugar
1 BUTTER FLAVOR* CRISCO® Stick or
1 cup BUTTER FLAVOR CRISCO
all-vegetable shortening
2 eggs
¼ cup light corn syrup or regular pancake
syrup
1 tablespoon vanilla
3 cups all-purpose flour plus
4 tablespoons, divided
¾ teaspoon baking powder
½ teaspoon baking soda
½ teaspoon salt
Decorations of your choice: granulated
sugar, colored sugar crystals,
frosting, decors, candies, chips, nuts,
raisins, decorating gel

*Butter Flavor Crisco is artificially flavored.

1. Combine sugar and shortening in large bowl. **Beat** at medium speed of electric mixer until well blended. **Add** eggs, syrup and vanilla. **Beat** until well blended and fluffy.

2. Combine 3 cups flour, baking powder, baking soda and salt. **Add** gradually to creamed mixture at low speed. **Mix** until well blended. **Divide** dough into 4 quarters.

3. Heat oven to 375°F. **Place** sheets of foil on countertop for cooling cookies.

4. Spread 1 tablespoon flour on large sheet of waxed paper. **Place** one-fourth of dough on floured paper. **Flatten** slightly with hands. **Turn** dough over and **cover** with another large sheet of waxed paper. **Roll** dough to ¼-inch thickness. **Remove** top sheet of waxed paper.

5. Cut out cookies with floured cutter. **Transfer** to ungreased baking sheet with large pancake turner. **Place** 2 inches apart. **Repeat** with remaining dough and flour. **Sprinkle** with granulated sugar, colored sugar crystals, decors or leave plain to frost or decorate when cooled.

6. Bake one baking sheet at a time at 375°F for 5 to 9 minutes, depending on the size of your cookies (bake smaller, thinner cookies closer to 5 minutes; larger cookies closer to 9 minutes). *Do not overbake.* **Cool** 2 minutes on baking sheet. **Remove** cookies to foil to cool completely, then **frost** if desired.

Makes about 3 to 4 dozen cookies

Tip: For well-defined cookie edges, or if dough is too sticky or too soft to roll, do the following. **Wrap** each quarter of dough with plastic wrap. **Refrigerate** 1 hour. **Keep** dough balls refrigerated until ready to roll.

Cream Cheese Cutout Cookies

1 **cup butter, softened**
1 **package (8 ounces) cream cheese,**
  softened
1½ **cups sugar**
1 **egg**
1 **teaspoon vanilla**
½ **teaspoon almond extract**
3½ **cups all-purpose flour**
1 **teaspoon baking powder**
  Almond Frosting (recipe follows)
  Assorted candies for decoration
  (optional)

In large bowl, beat butter and cream cheese until well combined. Add sugar; beat until fluffy. Add egg, vanilla and almond extract; beat well. In small bowl, combine flour and baking powder. Add dry ingredients to cream cheese mixture; beat until well mixed. Divide dough in half. Wrap each portion in plastic wrap; refrigerate about 1½ hours.

Preheat oven to 375°F. Roll out dough, half at a time, to ⅛-inch thickness on lightly floured surface. Cut out with cookie cutters. Place 2 inches apart on ungreased cookie sheets.

Bake 8 to 10 minutes or until edges are lightly browned. Remove to wire racks to cool completely. Frost cookies with Almond Frosting; decorate with assorted candies, if desired.

Makes about 7 dozen cookies

Almond Frosting: In small bowl, beat 2 cups sifted powdered sugar, 2 tablespoons softened butter and ¼ teaspoon almond extract until smooth. For piping consistency, beat in 4 to 5 teaspoons milk. For spreading consistency, add a little more milk. If desired, tint with food coloring.

Favorite recipe from **Wisconsin Milk Marketing Board**

Frosted Butter Cookies

COOKIES

1½ cups butter, softened
¾ cup granulated sugar
3 egg yolks
3 cups all-purpose flour
1 teaspoon baking powder
2 tablespoons orange juice
1 teaspoon vanilla extract

FROSTING

4 cups powdered sugar
½ cup butter, softened
3 to 4 tablespoons milk
2 teaspoons vanilla extract
Food coloring (optional)
Colored sugars, flaked coconut and
cinnamon candies for decoration

1. For Cookies, beat 1½ cups butter and granulated sugar in large bowl with electric mixer at medium speed until creamy. Add egg yolks; beat until light and fluffy. Add flour, baking powder, orange juice and 1 teaspoon vanilla; beat until well mixed. Cover; refrigerate 2 to 3 hours until firm.

2. Preheat oven to 350°F.

3. Roll out dough, ½ at a time, to ¼-inch thickness on well-floured surface. Cut out with holiday cookie cutters. Place, 1 inch apart, on ungreased cookie sheets. Bake 6 to 10 minutes until edges are golden brown. Remove to wire racks; cool completely.

4. For Frosting, combine all frosting ingredients
except food coloring and decorations in medium bowl;
beat until light and fluffy. If desired, divide frosting
into small bowls; tint with food coloring. Frost cookies
and decorate with colored sugars, coconut and candies.
Store tightly covered between sheets of waxed paper.

Makes about 3 dozen cookies

Cinnamon Stars

    2   tablespoons sugar
    ¾   teaspoon ground cinnamon
    ¾   cup butter or margarine, softened
    2   egg yolks
    1   teaspoon vanilla extract
    1   package DUNCAN HINES® Moist
        Deluxe French Vanilla Cake Mix

1. Preheat oven to 375°F.

2. Combine sugar and cinnamon in small bowl. Set
aside.

3. Combine butter, egg yolks and vanilla extract in
large bowl. Blend in cake mix gradually. Roll to ⅛-inch
thickness on lightly floured surface. Cut with 2½-inch
star cookie cutter. Place, 2 inches apart, on ungreased
baking sheets. Sprinkle cookies with cinnamon-sugar
mixture.

4. Bake at 375°F for 6 to 8 minutes or until edges are
light golden brown. Cool 1 minute on baking sheets.
Remove to cooling racks. Cool completely. Store in
airtight container.   *Makes 3 to 3½ dozen cookies*

Toffee Spattered Sugar Stars

1¼ cups granulated sugar
1 BUTTER FLAVOR* CRISCO® Stick or
    1 cup BUTTER FLAVOR CRISCO
    all-vegetable shortening
2 eggs
¼ cup light corn syrup or regular pancake
    syrup
1 tablespoon vanilla
3 cups all-purpose flour (plus
    4 tablespoons), divided
¾ teaspoon baking powder
½ teaspoon baking soda
½ teaspoon salt
1 package (6 ounces) milk chocolate
    English toffee chips, divided

*Butter Flavor Crisco is artificially flavored.

1. Place sugar and shortening in large bowl. **Beat** at medium speed of electric mixer until well blended. **Add** eggs, syrup and vanilla; beat until well blended and fluffy.

2. Combine 3 cups flour, baking powder, baking soda and salt. **Add** gradually to shortening mixture, beating at low speed until well blended.

3. Divide dough into 4 equal pieces; shape each into disk. **Wrap** with plastic wrap. **Refrigerate** 1 hour or until firm.

4. Heat oven to 375°F. **Place** sheets of foil on countertop for cooling cookies.

5. Sprinkle about 1 tablespoon flour on large sheet of waxed paper. **Place** disk of dough on floured paper; flatten slightly with hands. **Turn** dough over; cover with another large sheet of waxed paper. **Roll** dough to ¼-inch thickness. **Remove** top sheet of waxed paper. **Sprinkle** about ¼ of toffee chips over dough. **Roll** lightly into dough. **Cut** out with floured star or round cookie cutter. **Place** 2 inches apart on ungreased baking sheet. **Repeat** with remaining dough, flour and toffee chips.

6. Bake one baking sheet at a time at 375°F for 5 to 7 minutes or until cookies are lightly browned around edges. *Do not overbake.* **Cool** 2 minutes on baking sheet. **Remove** cookies to foil to cool completely.

Makes about 3½ dozen cookies

Frosted Easter Cut-outs

COOKIES

   1¼ cups granulated sugar

   1   BUTTER FLAVOR* CRISCO® Stick or
       1 cup BUTTER FLAVOR CRISCO
       all-vegetable shortening

   2   eggs

   ¼ cup light corn syrup or regular pancake
       syrup

   1   tablespoon vanilla

   3   cups all-purpose flour (plus
       4 tablespoons), divided

   ¾ teaspoon baking powder

   ½ teaspoon baking soda

   ½ teaspoon salt

ICING

   1   cup confectioners sugar

   2   tablespoons milk
       Food color (optional)
       Decorating icing

*Butter Flavor Crisco is artificially flavored.

1. Place sugar and shortening in large bowl. **Beat** at medium speed of electric mixer until well blended. **Add** eggs, syrup and vanilla; beat until well blended and fluffy.

2. Combine 3 cups flour, baking powder, baking soda and salt. **Add** gradually to shortening mixture, beating at low speed until well blended.

3. Divide dough into 4 equal pieces; shape each into disk. **Wrap** with plastic wrap. **Refrigerate** 1 hour or until firm.

4. Heat oven to 375°F. **Place** sheets of foil on countertop for cooling cookies.

5. Sprinkle about 1 tablespoon flour on large sheet of waxed paper. **Place** disk of dough on floured paper; flatten slightly with hands. **Turn** dough over; cover with another large sheet of waxed paper. **Roll** dough to ¼-inch thickness. **Remove** top sheet of waxed paper. **Cut** into desired shapes with floured cookie cutter. **Place** 2 inches apart on ungreased baking sheet. **Repeat** with remaining dough and flour.

6. Bake one baking sheet at a time at 375°F for 5 to 7 minutes or until edges of cookies are lightly browned. *Do not overbake.* **Cool** 2 minutes on baking sheet. **Remove** cookies to foil to cool completely.

7. *For icing*, combine confectioners sugar and milk; stir until smooth. **Add** food color, if desired. **Stir** until blended. **Spread** icing on cookies; place on foil until icing is set. **Decorate** as desired with decorating icing.

Makes about 3½ dozen cookies

Gingerbread Bears

3½ **cups all-purpose flour**
  2 **teaspoons ground cinnamon**
1½ **teaspoons ground ginger**
  1 **teaspoon salt**
  1 **teaspoon baking soda**
  1 **teaspoon ground allspice**
  1 **cup butter or margarine, softened**
  1 **cup firmly packed brown sugar**
  1 **teaspoon vanilla extract**
  ⅓ **cup molasses**
  2 **eggs**
   Assorted cookie nonpareils and colored
      sugar (optional)
   Ornamental Frosting (recipe follows)
      or **prepared creamy or gel-type**
      frostings in tubes (optional)
   Assorted candies and grated chocolate

1. Combine flour, cinnamon, ginger, salt, baking soda and allspice in medium bowl. Beat butter, sugar and vanilla in large bowl with electric mixer at medium speed about 5 minutes or until light and fluffy, scraping down side of bowl once. (Mixture will not be completely smooth.) Beat in molasses and eggs until well blended, scraping down side of bowl once.

2. Beat in flour mixture at low speed until well blended. Divide dough into 3 equal pieces. Flatten each piece of dough into a disc; wrap in plastic wrap. Refrigerate at least 2 hours or up to 24 hours.

3. Preheat oven to 350°F. Grease large cookie sheets.

4. Working with 1 piece of dough at a time, remove plastic wrap and place dough on lightly floured surface. Roll out dough with lightly floured rolling pin to ⅛-inch thickness. Keep remaining dough refrigerated.

5. Cut out dough with 3-inch bear-shaped cookie cutters. Place cookies 1 inch apart on prepared cookie sheets. Roll pieces of dough scraps into balls and ropes to make eyes, noses and to decorate bears. Decorate bears with nonpareils, if desired.

6. Bake 10 minutes or until bottoms of cookies are golden brown. Let stand on cookie sheet 1 minute. Remove cookies with spatula to wire rack; cool completely.

7. Prepare Ornamental Frosting, if desired. Pipe or spread frosting on cooled cookies. Decorate with assorted nonpareils, colored sugar, assorted candies and/or grated chocolate. Store tightly covered at room temperature.   *Makes about 3½ dozen cookies*

Ornamental Frosting

½ **cup butter or margarine, softened**
1 **teaspoon vanilla extract**
1 **package (16 ounces) powdered sugar, sifted**
2 **tablespoons milk**

Beat butter and vanilla in large bowl with electric mixer at medium speed, scraping down side of bowl once. Beat in powdered sugar and enough milk at low speed until frosting becomes desired spreading consistency.   *Makes about 2 cups frosting*

Peanut Butter Cut-Outs

½ cup SKIPPY® Creamy Peanut Butter
6 tablespoons MAZOLA® Margarine or
    butter, softened
½ cup packed brown sugar
⅓ cup KARO® Light or Dark Corn Syrup
1 egg
2 cups flour, divided
1½ teaspoons baking powder
1 teaspoon cinnamon (optional)
⅛ teaspoon salt

1. In large bowl with mixer at medium speed, beat
peanut butter, margarine, brown sugar, corn syrup and
egg until smooth. Reduce speed; beat in 1 cup flour,
baking powder, cinnamon and salt. With spoon stir in
remaining 1 cup flour.

2. Divide dough in half. Between two sheets of waxed
paper on large cookie sheets, roll each half of dough
¼ inch thick. Refrigerate until firm, about 1 hour.

3. Preheat oven to 350°F. Remove top piece of waxed
paper. With floured cookie cutters, cut dough into
shapes. Place on ungreased cookie sheets.

4. Bake 10 minutes or until lightly browned. Do not
overbake. Let stand on cookie sheets 2 minutes.
Remove from cookie sheets; cool completely on wire
racks. Reroll dough trimmings and cut. Decorate as
desired.   *Makes about 5 dozen cookies*

Gingerbread Cookies

½ cup vegetable shortening
⅓ cup packed light brown sugar
¼ cup dark molasses
1 egg white
½ teaspoon vanilla extract
1½ cups all-purpose flour
½ teaspoon baking soda
½ teaspoon salt
¼ teaspoon baking powder
1 teaspoon ground cinnamon
½ teaspoon ground ginger

1. Beat shortening, brown sugar, molasses, egg white and vanilla in large bowl with electric mixer at high speed until smooth. Combine flour, baking soda, salt, baking powder and spices in small bowl. Add to shortening mixture; mix well. Cover; refrigerate about 8 hours or overnight until firm.

2. Preheat oven to 350°F. Grease cookie sheets.

3. Roll out dough on lightly floured surface to ⅛-inch thickness. Cut into desired shapes with cookie cutters. Place on prepared cookie sheets.

4. Bake 6 to 8 minutes until edges begin to brown. Remove to wire racks; cool completely. Decorate as desired. Store tightly covered.

Makes about 2½ dozen cookies

Gingersnaps

2½ cups all-purpose flour
1½ teaspoons ground ginger
 1 teaspoon baking soda
 1 teaspoon ground allspice
 ½ teaspoon salt
1½ cups sugar
 2 tablespoons margarine, softened
 ½ cup MOTT'S® Apple Sauce
 ¼ cup GRANDMA'S® Molasses

1. Preheat oven to 375°F. Spray cookie sheet with nonstick cooking spray.

2. In medium bowl, sift together flour, ginger, baking soda, allspice and salt.

3. In large bowl, beat sugar and margarine with electric mixer at medium speed until blended. Whisk in apple sauce and molasses.

4. Add flour mixture to apple sauce mixture; stir until well blended.

5. Drop rounded tablespoonfuls of dough 1 inch apart onto prepared cookie sheet. Flatten each slightly with moistened fingertips.

6. Bake 12 to 15 minutes or until firm. Cool completely on wire rack.   *Makes 3 dozen cookies*

Yuletide Ginger Cookies

¾ cup firmly packed brown sugar
½ cup light corn syrup
½ cup (1 stick) margarine, softened
2 egg whites, slightly beaten
3 cups QUAKER® Oat Bran Hot Cereal, uncooked
¾ cup all-purpose flour
2 teaspoons ground ginger
1 teaspoon baking soda
1 teaspoon ground cinnamon
¼ cup red or green colored sugar crystals

Heat oven to 350°F. Beat brown sugar, corn syrup and margarine in medium bowl until fluffy. Blend in egg whites. In large bowl, combine oat bran, flour, ginger, baking soda and cinnamon. Gradually add brown sugar mixture; mix well. Shape into 1-inch balls; roll in colored sugar crystals to coat. Place 2 inches apart on ungreased cookie sheet. Gently press balls into 2-inch circles. Bake 11 to 13 minutes or until light golden brown. Cool 2 minutes on cookie sheet; remove to wire rack. Cool completely. Store tightly covered.

Makes about 3½ dozen cookies

Low Fat Molasses Jumbles

½ cup Prune Pureé (page 280) or
    prepared prune butter
½ cup sugar
½ cup molasses
1 egg
2 cups all-purpose flour
2 teaspoons ground cinnamon
1 teaspoon ground ginger
½ teaspoon baking soda
½ teaspoon salt
    Additional sugar

Preheat oven to 350°F. Coat baking sheets with
vegetable cooking spray. In large bowl, mix prune
purée, sugar and molasses until well blended. Add egg;
mix well. Combine remaining ingredients except sugar;
stir into prune purée mixture just until blended. Roll
heaping tablespoonfuls of dough in additional sugar.
Place on baking sheets, spacing 2 inches apart. With
fork, flatten dough in crisscross fashion until ½ inch
thick. Bake in center of oven about 12 to 13 minutes or
until set and bottoms are lightly browned. Remove
from baking sheets to wire racks to cool completely.

Makes 30 (2½-inch) cookies

Favorite recipe from **California Prune Board**

Honey Spice Balls

½ cup butter or margarine, softened
½ cup packed brown sugar
1 egg
1 tablespoon honey
1 teaspoon vanilla extract
2 cups all-purpose flour
½ teaspoon baking powder
½ teaspoon ground cinnamon
¼ teaspoon ground nutmeg
    Uncooked quick oats

1. Preheat oven to 350°F. Grease cookie sheets.

2. Beat butter and brown sugar in large bowl with electric mixer at medium speed until creamy. Add egg, honey and vanilla; beat until light and fluffy. Stir in flour, baking powder, cinnamon and nutmeg until well blended. Shape tablespoonfuls of dough into balls; roll in oats. Place 2 inches apart on prepared cookie sheets.

3. Bake 15 to 18 minutes until cookie tops crack slightly. Cool 1 minute on cookie sheets. Remove to wire racks; cool completely. Store tightly covered.

Makes about 2½ dozen cookies

Moist Pumpkin Cookies

½ cup butter or margarine, softened
1 cup packed brown sugar
½ cup granulated sugar
1½ cups canned pumpkin (not pumpkin pie filling)
1 egg
1 teaspoon vanilla extract
2¼ cups all-purpose flour
1¼ teaspoons ground cinnamon
1 teaspoon baking powder
½ teaspoon baking soda
½ teaspoon salt
½ teaspoon ground nutmeg
¾ cup raisins
½ cup chopped walnuts
Powdered Sugar Glaze (recipe follows)

1. Preheat oven to 350°F.

2. Beat butter and sugars in large bowl with electric mixer on medium speed until creamy. Beat in pumpkin, egg and vanilla until light and fluffy. Mix in flour, cinnamon, baking powder, baking soda, salt and nutmeg until blended. Stir in raisins and walnuts. Drop heaping tablespoonfuls of dough 2 inches apart onto ungreased cookie sheets.

3. Bake 12 to 15 minutes until set. Cool 2 minutes on cookie sheets. Remove to wire racks; cool completely. Drizzle Powdered Sugar Glaze onto cookies. Let glaze set. Store between layers of waxed paper in airtight containers.   *Makes about 3½ dozen cookies*

Powdered Sugar Glaze: Combine 1 cup powdered sugar and 2 tablespoons milk in small bowl until well blended.

Cranberry Nut Oatmeal Cookies

1¼ cups firmly packed light brown sugar
¾ BUTTER FLAVOR* CRISCO® Stick or
   ¾ cup BUTTER FLAVOR CRISCO
   all-vegetable shortening
1 egg
⅓ cup milk
1½ teaspoons vanilla
1 teaspoon grated orange peel
3 cups quick oats, uncooked
1 cup all-purpose flour
½ teaspoon baking soda
½ teaspoon salt
¼ teaspoon cinnamon
1 cup dried cranberries
1 cup coarsely chopped walnuts

*Butter Flavor Crisco is artificially flavored.

1. Heat oven to 375°F. **Grease** baking sheets. **Place** sheets of foil on countertop for cooling cookies.

2. Place brown sugar, shortening, egg, milk, vanilla and orange peel in large bowl. **Beat** at medium speed of electric mixer until well blended.

3. Combine oats, flour, baking soda, salt and cinnamon. **Add** to shortening mixture; beat at low speed just until blended. **Stir** in cranberries and walnuts.

4. Drop dough by rounded measuring tablespoonfuls 2 inches apart onto prepared baking sheets.

5. Bake one baking sheet at a time at 375°F for 10 to 12 minutes or until cookies are lightly browned. *Do not overbake.* **Cool** 2 minutes on baking sheet. **Remove** cookies to foil to cool completely.

Makes about 2½ dozen cookies

Pumpkin Cheesecake Bars

BASE AND TOPPING

- 2 cups all-purpose flour
- ⅔ cup packed light brown sugar
- ½ cup (1 stick) butter or margarine
- 1 cup finely chopped pecans

PUMPKIN CREAM CHEESE FILLING

- 11 ounces (*one* 8-ounce package and *one* 3-ounce package) cream cheese, softened
- 1¼ cups granulated sugar
- 1½ teaspoons vanilla extract
- 1½ teaspoons ground cinnamon
- ½ teaspoon ground allspice
- ¾ cup LIBBY'S® Solid Pack Pumpkin
- 3 eggs
  Glazed Pecans (recipe follows)

FOR BASE AND TOPPING:

COMBINE flour and brown sugar in medium bowl. Cut in butter with pastry blender or two knives until mixture resembles coarse crumbs; stir in nuts. Reserve *1½ cups* mixture for topping; press remaining mixture onto bottom of ungreased 13×9-inch baking pan. Bake in preheated 350°F. oven for 15 minutes.

FOR PUMPKIN CREAM CHEESE FILLING:

BEAT cream cheese, granulated sugar, vanilla, cinnamon and allspice in large mixer bowl until smooth. Beat in pumpkin and eggs. Spread over crust; sprinkle with *reserved* topping. Bake in 350°F. oven for 25 to 30 minutes or until center is set. Cool in pan on wire rack; chill for several hours or until firm. Cut into bars; place Glazed Pecan half on each bar.

Makes 32 bar cookies

FOR GLAZED PECANS:

PLACE waxed paper under greased wire rack. Bring ¼ cup dark corn syrup to a boil in medium saucepan; boil, stirring occasionally, for 1 minute. Remove from heat; stir in 30 pecan halves. Remove pecan halves to wire rack. Turn right side up; separate. Cool.

Cranberry Orange Ricotta Cheese Brownies

CHEESE FILLING
- 1 cup ricotta cheese
- 3 tablespoons whole-berry cranberry sauce
- ¼ cup sugar
- 1 egg
- 2 tablespoons cornstarch
- ¼ to ½ teaspoon grated orange peel
- 4 drops red food color (optional)

BROWNIES
- ½ cup butter or margarine, melted
- ¾ cup sugar
- 1 teaspoon vanilla extract
- 2 eggs
- ¾ cup all-purpose flour
- ½ cup HERSHEY₀S Cocoa
- ½ teaspoon baking powder
- ½ teaspoon salt

Heat oven to 350°F. Grease 9-inch square baking pan.

To prepare Cheese Filling, in small bowl, beat ricotta cheese, cranberry sauce, ¼ cup sugar, 1 egg and cornstarch until smooth. Stir in orange peel and food color, if desired. Set aside.

To prepare Brownies, in another small bowl, stir together melted butter, ¾ cup sugar and vanilla; add 2 eggs, beating well. Stir together flour, cocoa, baking powder and salt; add to butter mixture, mixing thoroughly. Spread half of cocoa batter in prepared pan. Spread Cheese Filling over top. Drop remaining cocoa batter by teaspoonfuls onto Cheese Filling. Bake 40 to 45 minutes or until wooden pick inserted in center comes out clean. Cool completely in pan on wire rack. Cut into squares; refrigerate.

Makes about 16 brownies

Cranberry Walnut Bars

Bar Cookie Crust (page 252)
2   eggs
½   cup KARO® Light or Dark Corn Syrup
½   cup sugar
2   tablespoons MAZOLA® Margarine or
     butter, melted
1   cup dried cranberries or raisins (about
     6 ounces)
¾   cup chopped walnuts

1. Preheat oven to 350°F. Prepare Bar Cookie Crust.

2. Meanwhile, in medium bowl beat eggs, corn syrup, sugar and margarine until well blended. Stir in cranberries and walnuts. Pour over hot crust; spread evenly.

3. Bake 15 to 18 minutes or until set. Cool completely on wire rack. Cut into 2×1½-inch bars.

Makes about 32 bars

German Honey Bars (Lebkuchen)

2¾ cups all-purpose flour
2 teaspoons ground cinnamon
1 teaspoon baking powder
½ teaspoon baking soda
½ teaspoon salt
½ teaspoon ground cardamom
½ teaspoon ground ginger
½ cup honey
½ cup dark molasses
¾ cup packed brown sugar
3 tablespoons butter, melted
1 large egg
½ cup chopped toasted almonds (optional)
Glaze (recipe follows)

1. Preheat oven to 350°F. Grease 15×10-inch jelly-roll pan.

2. Combine flour, cinnamon, baking powder, baking soda, salt, cardamom and ginger in medium bowl; set aside.

3. Combine honey and molasses in medium saucepan; bring to a boil over medium heat. Remove from heat; cool 10 minutes.

4. Stir in brown sugar, butter and egg. Place brown sugar mixture in large bowl. Gradually add flour mixture. Beat at low speed with electric mixer until dough forms, scraping down side of bowl once. Stir in almonds with spoon, if desired. (Dough will be slightly sticky.)

5. Spread dough evenly into prepared pan. Bake 20 to 22 minutes until golden brown and set. Remove pan to wire rack; cool completely.

6. Prepare Glaze. Spread over cooled bar cookies. Let stand until set, about 30 minutes.

7. Cut into 2×1-inch bars. Store tightly covered at room temperature or freeze up to 3 months.

Makes about 6 dozen bars

Glaze

1¼ **cups powdered sugar**
3 **tablespoons fresh lemon juice**
1 **teaspoon grated lemon peel**

Place all ingredients in medium bowl; stir with spoon until smooth.

Yuletide Toffee Squares

4½ cups quick or old-fashioned oats
1 cup packed brown sugar
¾ cup (1½ sticks) butter or margarine, melted
½ cup light corn syrup
1 tablespoon vanilla extract
½ teaspoon salt
2 cups (12-ounce package) NESTLÉ® TOLL HOUSE® Semi-Sweet Chocolate Morsels
⅔ cup chopped nuts

COMBINE oats, brown sugar, butter, corn syrup, vanilla and salt in large bowl; mix well. Firmly press mixture into greased 15½×10½-inch jelly-roll pan.

BAKE in preheated 400°F. oven for 18 minutes or until mixture is browned and bubbly. Remove from oven. Immediately sprinkle chocolate morsels evenly over toffee. Let stand 10 minutes.

SPREAD chocolate evenly over toffee; sprinkle with nuts. Cool completely; cut into squares. Store tightly covered in cool, dry place.

Makes 6 dozen squares

Gooey Caramel Chocolate Bars

2 cups all-purpose flour
1 cup granulated sugar
¼ teaspoon salt
2 cups butter or margarine, divided
1 cup packed light brown sugar
⅓ cup light corn syrup
1 cup (6 ounces) semisweet chocolate chips

1. Preheat oven to 350°F. Line 13×9-inch baking pan with foil.

2. Combine flour, granulated sugar and salt in medium bowl. Cut in 14 tablespoons (1¾ sticks) butter until mixture resembles coarse crumbs. Press into bottom of prepared pan.

3. Bake 18 to 20 minutes until lightly browned around edges. Remove pan to wire rack; cool completely.

4. Combine 1 cup butter, brown sugar and corn syrup in heavy medium saucepan. Cook over medium heat 5 to 8 minutes until mixture boils, stirring frequently. Boil gently 2 minutes, without stirring. Immediately pour over cooled base; spread evenly to edges of pan with metal spatula. Cool completely.

5. Melt chocolate in double boiler over hot, not boiling, water. Stir in remaining 2 tablespoons butter. Pour over cooled caramel layer and spread evenly to edges of pan with metal spatula. Refrigerate 10 to 15 minutes until chocolate begins to set. Remove; cool completely. Cut into bars. Store tightly covered.

Makes 3 dozen bars

Walnut-Brandy Shortbread

- 1 **cup butter**
- ½ **cup packed brown sugar**
- ⅛ **teaspoon salt**
- 2 **tablespoons brandy**
- 1 **cup all-purpose flour**
- 1 **cup finely chopped toasted California walnuts**
  Granulated sugar

Cream butter with brown sugar and salt in large bowl; mix in brandy. Gradually add flour; stir in walnuts. Spread in ungreased 9-inch square pan. Refrigerate 30 minutes.

Pierce mixture all over with fork. Bake at 325°F about 55 minutes or until dark golden brown. If dough puffs up during baking, pierce again with fork. Sprinkle lightly with granulated sugar and cool. Cut into squares with sharp knife.   *Makes 36 squares*

Favorite recipe from **Walnut Marketing Board**

Linzer Bars

¾ cup butter or margarine, softened
½ cup sugar
1 egg
½ teaspoon grated lemon peel
½ teaspoon ground cinnamon
¼ teaspoon salt
⅛ teaspoon ground cloves
2 cups all-purpose flour
1 cup DIAMOND® Walnuts, finely
    chopped or ground
1 cup raspberry or apricot jam

Preheat oven to 325°F. Grease 9-inch square pan. In
large bowl, cream butter, sugar, egg, lemon peel,
cinnamon, salt and cloves. Blend in flour and walnuts.
Set aside about ¼ of the dough for lattice top. Pat
remaining dough into bottom and about ½ inch up
sides of pan. Spread with jam. Make pencil-shaped strips
of remaining dough, rolling against floured board with
palms of hands. Arrange in lattice pattern over top,
pressing ends against dough on sides. Bake 45 minutes
or until lightly browned. Cool in pan on wire rack. Cut
into bars. *Makes 2 dozen small bars*

Linzer Sandwich Cookies

1⅓ cups all-purpose flour
¼   teaspoon baking powder
¼   teaspoon salt
¾   cup sugar
½   cup butter, softened
1   large egg
1   teaspoon vanilla extract
    Seedless raspberry jam

1. Combine flour, baking powder and salt in small bowl. Beat sugar and butter in medium bowl with electric mixer at medium speed until light and fluffy, scraping down side of bowl once. Beat in egg and vanilla. Gradually add flour mixture. Beat at low speed until dough forms, scraping down side of bowl once. Form dough into 2 discs; wrap in plastic wrap and refrigerate 2 hours or until firm.

2. Preheat oven to 375°F.

3. Working with 1 disc at a time, unwrap dough and place on lightly floured surface. Roll out dough with lightly floured rolling pin. Cut dough into desired shapes with floured cookie cutters. Cut out equal numbers of each shape. (If dough becomes too soft, refrigerate several minutes before continuing.)

4. Cut 1-inch centers out of half the cookies of each shape. Gently press dough trimmings together; reroll and cut out more cookies. Place cookies 1½ to 2 inches apart on ungreased cookie sheets.

5. Bake 7 to 9 minutes until edges are lightly brown. Let cookies stand on cookie sheets 1 to 2 minutes. Remove cookies with spatula to wire racks; cool completely.

6. Spread 1 teaspoon jam on flat side of whole cookies, spreading almost to edges. Place cookies with holes, flat sides down, over jam. Store tightly covered at room temperature or freeze up to 3 months.

Makes about 2 dozen cookies

Best-Ever

BARS

Luscious Lemon Bars

  2 **cups all-purpose flour**
  1 **cup butter**
  ½ **cup powdered sugar**
  4 **teaspoons lemon peel, divided**
  ¼ **teaspoon salt**
  1 **cup granulated sugar**
  3 **large eggs**
  ⅓ **cup fresh lemon juice**
     Sifted powdered sugar

1. Preheat oven to 350°F. Grease 13×9-inch baking pan.

2. Place flour, butter, ½ cup powdered sugar, 1 teaspoon lemon peel and salt in food processor. Process until mixture forms coarse crumbs. Press mixture evenly into prepared pan.

3. Bake 18 to 20 minutes until golden brown. Beat remaining 3 teaspoons lemon peel, granulated sugar, eggs and lemon juice in medium bowl with electric mixer at medium speed until well blended. Pour over warm crust. Return to oven; bake 18 to 20 minutes until center is set and edges are golden brown. Remove pan to wire rack; cool completely. Dust with sifted powdered sugar; cut into 2×1½-inch bars. Store tightly covered at room temperature. *Do not freeze.*

Makes 3 dozen bars

Zesty Fresh Lemon Bars

CRUST

- ½ cup butter or margarine, softened
- ½ cup granulated sugar
  Grated peel of ½ SUNKIST® Lemon
- 1¼ cups all-purpose flour

FILLING

- 1 cup packed brown sugar
- 1 cup chopped walnuts
- 2 eggs, slightly beaten
- ¼ cup all-purpose flour
  Grated peel of ½ SUNKIST® Lemon
- ¼ teaspoon baking powder

GLAZE

- 1 cup powdered sugar
- 1 tablespoon butter, softened
- 2 tablespoons fresh-squeezed SUNKIST®
  Lemon Juice

To prepare crust: Preheat oven to 350°F. In bowl, beat butter, granulated sugar and lemon peel. Gradually stir in flour to form soft dough. Press on bottom of ungreased 13×9×2-inch pan. Bake 15 minutes.

To prepare filling: In medium bowl, combine all filling ingredients. Spread over baked crust. Bake 20 minutes. Meanwhile, prepare glaze.

To prepare glaze: In small bowl, gradually blend small amount of powdered sugar into butter. Add lemon juice and remaining powdered sugar; stir to blend well. Drizzle over hot lemon filling. Cool in pan on wire rack; cut into bars.   *Makes about 3 dozen bars*

PHILLY® FREE® Lemon Bars

1   cup flour
½   cup firmly packed brown sugar
¼   cup granulated sugar
½   cup (1 stick) reduced-fat tablespread,
      cold
1   cup old-fashioned or quick-cooking
      oats, uncooked
1   package (8 ounces) PHILADELPHIA
      BRAND® FREE® Fat Free Cream
      Cheese, softened
1   egg
¼   cup lemon juice
1   tablespoon grated lemon peel

MIX flour and sugars; cut in tablespread until mixture
resembles coarse crumbs. Stir in oats. Reserve 1 cup of
the crumb mixture. Press remaining crumb mixture
onto bottom of 9-inch square baking pan that has been
sprayed with nonstick cooking spray.

BAKE at 350°F for 20 minutes.

BEAT cream cheese with electric mixer on medium
speed until smooth. Add egg, juice and peel, mixing
until blended. Pour over crust; sprinkle with reserved 1
cup crumb mixture.

BAKE at 350°F for 25 minutes. Cool. Cut into bars or
triangles.   *Makes 16 bars*

Strawberry Streusel Bars

CRUMB MIXTURE
  2 **cups all-purpose flour**
  1 **cup sugar**
  ¾ **cup pecans, coarsely chopped**
  1 **cup butter or margarine, softened**
  1 **egg**
FILLING
  1 **jar (10 ounces) strawberry preserves**

1. Preheat oven to 350°F. Grease 9-inch square baking pan.

2. For crumb mixture, beat flour, sugar, pecans, butter and egg in large mixer bowl with electric mixer at low speed 2 to 3 minutes until mixture is crumbly, scraping bowl often. Reserve 1 cup crumb mixture; press remaining crumb mixture onto bottom of prepared baking pan. Spread preserves to within ½ inch of edge of unbaked crumb mixture. Crumble remaining crumb mixture over preserves.

3. Bake 42 to 50 minutes until lightly browned. Cool completely. Cut into bars. Store tightly covered.

Makes about 24 bars

SMUCKER'S® Crimson Ribbon Bars

6   **tablespoons butter or margarine, softened**
½   **cup firmly packed brown sugar**
1   **teaspoon vanilla**
½   **cup all-purpose flour**
¼   **teaspoon baking soda**
1½   **cups rolled oats**
1   **cup chopped walnuts**
½   **cup chopped BLUE RIBBON® Calimyrna or Mission Figs**
⅓   **cup SMUCKER'S® Red Raspberry Preserves**

Heat oven to 375°F. Combine butter, brown sugar and vanilla; beat until well blended. Add flour and baking soda; mix well. Stir in oats and walnuts. Reserve ¾ cup mixture for topping. Press remaining oat mixture in 8-inch square baking pan. Combine figs and preserves; spread mixture to within ½ inch of edges. Sprinkle with reserved oat mixture; press lightly.

Bake for 25 to 30 minutes or until golden brown. Cool in pan; cut into bars.   *Makes 20 bars*

Choco-Lowfat Strawberry Shortbread Bars

¼ cup (½ stick) 60% vegetable oil spread
½ cup sugar
1 egg white
1¼ cups all-purpose flour
¼ cup HERSHEY₀'S Cocoa or
    HERSHEY₀'S European Style Cocoa
¾ teaspoon cream of tartar
½ teaspoon baking soda
    Dash salt
½ cup strawberry all-fruit spread
    White Chip Drizzle (recipe follows)

Heat oven to 375°F. Lightly spray 13×9×2-inch baking pan with vegetable cooking spray. In medium bowl, combine vegetable oil spread and sugar; beat on medium speed of electric mixer until well blended. Add egg white; beat until well blended. Stir together flour, cocoa, cream of tartar, baking soda and salt; gradually add to sugar mixture, beating well. Gently press mixture onto bottom of prepared pan. Bake 10 to 12 minutes or just until set. Cool completely in pan on wire rack. Spread fruit spread evenly over crust. Cut into bars. Prepare White Chip Drizzle; drizzle over tops of bars. Let stand until set.　　　*Makes 36 bars*

White Chip Drizzle

⅓ cup HERSHEY₅S Premier White Chips
½ teaspoon shortening (do *not* use butter,
      margarine or oil)

In small microwave-safe bowl, place white chips and
shortening. Microwave at HIGH (100%) 30 seconds;
stir. If necessary, microwave at HIGH an additional 15
seconds at a time, stirring after each heating, just until
chips are melted when stirred. Use immediately.

Peanut Butter Chips and Jelly Bars

1½ cups all-purpose flour
½ cup sugar
¾ teaspoon baking powder
½ cup (1 stick) cold butter or margarine
1 egg, beaten
¾ cup grape jelly
1⅔ cups (10-ounce package) REESE'S®
      Peanut Butter Chips, divided

Heat oven to 375°F. Grease 9-inch square baking pan.
Stir together flour, sugar and baking powder; cut in
butter with pastry blender until mixture resembles
coarse crumbs. Add egg; blend well. Reserve half of
mixture; press remaining mixture onto bottom of
prepared pan. Spread jelly over crust. Sprinkle 1 cup
peanut butter chips over jelly. Stir together reserved
crumb mixture with remaining ⅔ cup chips; sprinkle
over top. Bake 25 to 30 minutes or until lightly
browned. Cool completely in pan on wire rack. Cut
into bars.   *Makes about 16 bars*

Four-Layer Oatmeal Bars

OAT LAYER

- ½ BUTTER FLAVOR* CRISCO® Stick or ½ cup BUTTER FLAVOR CRISCO all-vegetable shortening
- 1 egg
- 1½ cups quick oats, uncooked
- 1 cup firmly packed brown sugar
- ¾ cup plus 2 tablespoons all-purpose flour
- 1 teaspoon cinnamon
- ¾ teaspoon baking soda
- ¼ teaspoon salt

FRUIT LAYER

- 1½ cups sliced, peeled fresh peaches** (cut slices in half crosswise)
- ¾ cup crushed pineapple, undrained
- ¾ cup sliced, peeled Granny Smith apple (cut slices in half crosswise)
- ½ cup chopped walnuts or pecans
- ¼ cup granulated sugar
- 2 tablespoons cornstarch
- ½ teaspoon nutmeg

CREAM CHEESE LAYER

- 1 (8-ounce) package cream cheese, softened
- 1 egg
- ¼ cup granulated sugar
- ½ teaspoon fresh lemon juice
- ½ teaspoon vanilla

1. Heat oven to 350°F. **Grease** 11×7-inch glass baking dish with shortening. **Place** cooling rack on countertop.

2. *For oat layer*, combine shortening and egg in large bowl. **Stir** with fork until blended. **Add** oats, brown sugar, flour, cinnamon, baking soda and salt. **Stir** until well blended and crumbs form. **Press** 1¾ cups crumbs lightly into bottom of prepared dish. **Reserve** remaining crumbs.

3. Bake at 350°F for 10 minutes. *Do not overbake*. **Cool** completely on cooling rack.

4. *For fruit layer*, combine peaches, pineapple, apple, nuts, granulated sugar, cornstarch and nutmeg in medium saucepan. **Cook** and stir over medium heat until mixture comes to a boil and thickens. **Cool** completely.

5. *Increase oven temperature to 375°F.*

6. *For cream cheese layer*, combine cream cheese, egg, granulated sugar, lemon juice and vanilla in medium bowl. **Beat** at medium speed of electric mixer until well blended. **Spread** over cooled oat layer. **Spoon** cooled fruit mixture over cheese layer. **Spread** gently to cover cream cheese. **Sprinkle** reserved crumbs over fruit.

7. Bake at 375°F for 30 minutes. *Do not overbake*. **Cool** completely on cooling rack. **Refrigerate. Cut** into bars about 2×1¾ inches.   *Makes about 20 bars*

*Butter Flavor Crisco is artificially flavored.

**Diced canned peaches, well drained, can be used in place of fresh peaches.

Fruit and Chocolate Dream Bars

CRUST
- 1¼ cups all-purpose flour
- ½ cup granulated sugar
- ½ cup (1 stick) butter or margarine

TOPPING
- ⅔ cup all-purpose flour
- ½ cup chopped pecans
- ⅓ cup packed brown sugar
- 6 tablespoons (¾ stick) butter or margarine, softened
- ½ cup raspberry or strawberry jam
- 2 cups (11.5-ounce package) NESTLÉ® TOLL HOUSE® Milk Chocolate Morsels

FOR CRUST:
COMBINE flour and granulated sugar in medium bowl. Cut in butter with pastry blender or two knives until mixture resembles coarse crumbs. Press onto bottom of greased 9-inch-square baking pan. Bake in preheated 375°F. oven for 18 to 22 minutes or until set but not brown.

FOR TOPPING (prepare while crust is baking):
COMBINE flour, nuts and brown sugar in same bowl. Cut in butter with pastry blender or two knives until mixture resembles coarse crumbs.

SPREAD jam over hot crust. Sprinkle with morsels and Topping. Bake at 375°F. oven for 15 to 20 minutes or until golden brown. Cool completely in pan on wire rack. *Makes 2½ dozen bars*

O'Henrietta Bars

½ cup (1 stick) MAZOLA® Margarine or
    butter, softened
½ cup packed brown sugar
½ cup KARO® Light or Dark Corn Syrup
1 teaspoon vanilla
3 cups quick oats, uncooked
½ cup (3 ounces) semisweet chocolate
    chips
¼ cup SKIPPY® Creamy Peanut Butter

1. Preheat oven to 350°F. Grease 8- or 9-inch square
baking pan.

2. In large bowl with mixer at medium speed, beat
margarine, brown sugar, corn syrup and vanilla until
smooth. Stir in oats. Press into prepared pan.

3. Bake 25 minutes or until center is barely firm. Cool
on wire rack 5 minutes.

4. Sprinkle with chocolate chips; top with small
spoonfuls of peanut butter. Let stand 5 minutes; with
tip of knife, spread peanut butter and chocolate over
bars, swirling to marbleize. Cool completely on wire
rack before cutting. Cut into bars; refrigerate 15
minutes to set topping.   *Makes 24 bars*

Apple Crumb Squares

2 cups QUAKER® Oats (Quick or Old
Fashioned), uncooked
1½ cups all-purpose flour
1 cup packed brown sugar
¾ cup butter or margarine, melted
1 teaspoon ground cinnamon
½ teaspoon baking soda
½ teaspoon salt (optional)
¼ teaspoon ground nutmeg
1 cup applesauce
½ cup chopped nuts

Preheat oven to 350°F. In large bowl, combine all
ingredients except applesauce and nuts; mix until
crumbly. Reserve 1 cup oats mixture. Press remaining
mixture on bottom of greased 13×9-inch pan. Bake 13
to 15 minutes; cool. Spread applesauce over partially
baked crust; sprinkle with nuts. Sprinkle reserved 1
cup oats mixture over top. Bake 13 to 15 minutes or
until golden brown. Cool in pan on wire rack; cut into
2-inch squares.   *Makes about 24 squares*

Apple Macadamia Nut Bars

3　Golden Delicious apples, coarsely
　　chopped
1　tablespoon lemon juice
1　(16-ounce) package pound cake mix
1　cup milk
1　teaspoon grated lemon peel
½　teaspoon almond extract
1　cup flaked, sweetened coconut
3½　ounces macadamia nuts, coarsely
　　chopped
3½　ounces white chocolate, coarsely
　　chopped

1. Heat oven to 350°F. Grease and flour 13×9-inch baking pan. Combine apples and lemon juice; set aside.

2. In large bowl, with electric mixer, beat together pound cake mix, milk, lemon peel and almond extract. Stir in coconut, macadamia nuts, white chocolate and the reserved apples; mix well.

3. Spoon batter into prepared pan. Bake 50 to 55 minutes or until center springs back when gently pressed. Cool in pan 5 minutes; cut into bars.

Makes 12 bars

Favorite recipe from **Washington Apple Commission**

Fabulous Fruit Bars

1½ cups all-purpose flour, divided
1½ cups sugar, divided
½ cup MOTT'S® Apple Sauce, divided
½ teaspoon baking powder
2 tablespoons margarine
½ cup peeled, chopped apple
½ cup chopped dried apricots
½ cup chopped cranberries
1 whole egg
1 egg white
1 teaspoon lemon juice
½ teaspoon vanilla extract
1 teaspoon ground cinnamon

1. Preheat oven to 350°F. Spray 13×9-inch baking pan with nonstick cooking spray.

2. In medium bowl, combine 1¼ cups flour, ½ cup sugar, ⅓ cup apple sauce and baking powder. Cut in margarine with pastry blender or fork until mixture resembles coarse crumbs.

3. In large bowl, combine apple, apricots, cranberries, remaining apple sauce, whole egg, egg white, lemon juice and vanilla.

4. In small bowl, combine remaining 1 cup sugar, ¼ cup flour and cinnamon. Add to fruit mixture, stirring just until mixed.

5. Press half of crumb mixture evenly into bottom of prepared pan. Top with fruit mixture. Sprinkle with remaining crumb mixture.

6. Bake 40 minutes or until lightly browned. Broil, 4 inches from heat, 1 to 2 minutes or until golden brown. Cool on wire rack 15 minutes; cut into 16 bars.

Makes 16 bars

Pear Blondies

1 **cup packed brown sugar**
¼ **cup butter or margarine, melted**
1 **egg**
½ **teaspoon vanilla**
¾ **cup all-purpose flour**
½ **teaspoon baking powder**
½ **teaspoon salt**
1 **cup chopped firm-ripe fresh U.S.A. Anjou, Bosc, Bartlett, Nelis or Seckel pears**
⅓ **cup semisweet chocolate chips**

Preheat oven to 350°F. Grease 8-inch square baking pan.

Combine brown sugar, butter, egg and vanilla in medium bowl; blend well. Combine flour, baking powder and salt in small bowl; stir into brown sugar mixture. Stir in pears and chips. Spread in prepared baking pan. Bake 30 to 35 minutes or until golden brown. Cool completely in pan on wire rack. Cut into 2-inch squares.   *Makes 16 squares*

Favorite recipe from **Oregon Washington California Pear Bureau**

Cocoa Banana Bars

BARS

- ⅔ cup QUAKER® Oat Bran hot cereal, uncooked
- ⅔ cup all-purpose flour
- ½ cup granulated sugar
- ⅓ cup unsweetened cocoa
- ½ cup mashed ripe banana (about 1 large)
- ¼ cup liquid vegetable oil margarine
- 3 tablespoons light corn syrup
- 2 egg whites, slightly beaten
- 1 teaspoon vanilla

GLAZE

- 2 teaspoons unsweetened cocoa
- 2 teaspoons liquid vegetable oil margarine
- ¼ cup powdered sugar
- 2 to 2½ teaspoons warm water, divided
  Strawberry halves (optional)

For Bars, heat oven to 350°F. Lightly spray 8-inch square baking pan with nonstick cooking spray, or oil lightly. In large bowl, combine oat bran, flour, granulated sugar and ⅓ cup cocoa. Add combined banana, ¼ cup margarine, corn syrup, egg whites and vanilla; mix well. Pour into prepared pan, spreading evenly. Bake 23 to 25 minutes or until center is set. Cool on wire rack.

For Glaze, in small bowl combine 2 teaspoons cocoa and 2 teaspoons margarine. Stir in powdered sugar and 1 teaspoon of the water. Gradually add remaining 1 to 1½ teaspoons water to make medium-thick glaze, mixing well. Drizzle Glaze over brownies. Top with strawberry halves, if desired. Cut into bars. Store tightly covered.   *Makes 9 bars*

Banana Cocoa Marbled Bars

½ **cup uncooked rolled oats**
1½ **cups all-purpose flour**
2 **teaspoons baking powder**
½ **teaspoon baking soda**
½ **teaspoon salt**
1 **cup sugar**
½ **cup MOTT'S® Natural Apple Sauce**
1 **whole egg**
1 **egg white**
2 **tablespoons vegetable oil**
⅓ **cup low fat buttermilk**
2 **tablespoons unsweetened cocoa powder**
1 **large ripe banana, mashed (⅔ cup)**

1. Preheat oven to 350°F. Spray 9-inch square baking pan with nonstick cooking spray.

2. Place oats in food processor or blender; process until finely ground.

3. In medium bowl, combine oats, flour, baking powder, baking soda and salt.

4. In large bowl, combine sugar, apple sauce, whole egg, egg white and oil.

5. Add flour mixture to apple sauce mixture; stir until well blended. (Mixture will look dry.)

6. Remove 1 cup of batter to small bowl. Add buttermilk and cocoa; mix well.

7. Add banana to remaining batter. Mix well; spread into prepared pan.

8. Drop tablespoonfuls of cocoa batter over banana batter. Run knife through batters to marble.

9. Bake 35 minutes or until toothpick inserted in center comes out clean. Cool on wire rack 15 minutes; cut into 14 bars.   *Makes 14 bars*

Blueberry Cheesecake Bars

1 package DUNCAN HINES® Bakery Style
   Blueberry Muffin Mix
¼ cup cold butter or margarine
⅓ cup finely chopped pecans
1 (8-ounce) package cream cheese,
   softened
½ cup sugar
1 egg
3 tablespoons lemon juice
1 teaspoon grated lemon peel

1. Preheat oven to 350°F. Grease 9-inch square pan.

2. Rinse blueberries from Mix with cold water and drain.

3. Place muffin mix in medium bowl; cut in butter with pastry blender or two knives. Stir in pecans. Press into bottom of prepared pan. Bake 15 minutes or until set.

4. Combine cream cheese and sugar in medium bowl. Beat until smooth. Add egg, lemon juice and lemon peel. Beat well. Spread over baked crust. Sprinkle with blueberries. Sprinkle topping packet from Mix over blueberries. Return to oven. Bake 35 to 40 minutes or until filling is set. Cool completely. Refrigerate until ready to serve. Cut into bars.   *Makes about 16 bars*

Choco Cheesecake Squares

⅓ cup butter or margarine, softened
⅓ cup packed light brown sugar
1 cup plus 1 tablespoon all-purpose flour,
     divided
½ cup chopped pecans (optional)
1 cup semisweet chocolate chips
1 package (8 ounces) cream cheese,
     softened
¼ cup granulated sugar
1 egg
1 teaspoon vanilla extract

1. Preheat oven to 350°F. Grease 8-inch square
baking pan.

2. Beat butter and brown sugar in large bowl with
electric mixer at medium speed until light and fluffy.
Add 1 cup flour. Beat until well combined. Stir in nuts,
if desired. (Mixture will be crumbly.) Press evenly into
prepared pan. Bake 15 minutes.

3. Place chocolate chips in 1-cup glass measuring cup.
Melt in microwave oven at HIGH 2½ to 3 minutes,
stirring after 2 minutes. Beat cream cheese and
granulated sugar in medium bowl until light and fluffy.
Add remaining 1 tablespoon flour, egg and vanilla; beat
until smooth. Gradually stir in melted chocolate,
mixing well. Pour cream cheese mixture over partially
baked crust. Bake 15 minutes more or until set.
Remove pan to wire rack; cool completely. Cut into
2-inch squares. Store tightly covered.

Makes about 16 squares

Fudge Cheesecake Bars

4 bars (1 ounce each) HERSHEY'S
  Unsweetened Baking Chocolate,
  broken into pieces
1 cup (2 sticks) butter or margarine
2½ cups sugar, divided
4 eggs
1 teaspoon vanilla extract
2 cups all-purpose flour
1 package (8 ounces) cream cheese,
  softened
1 package (13 ounces) HERSHEY'S
  HUGS® Chocolates or HUGS WITH
  ALMONDS® Chocolates, divided

Heat oven to 350°F. Grease 13×9×2-inch baking pan.
In large microwave-safe bowl, place baking chocolate
and butter. Microwave at HIGH (100%) 2 to 2½
minutes, or until butter and chocolate are completely
melted, stirring after each minute. Beat in 2 cups
sugar, 3 eggs and vanilla until blended. Stir in flour;
spread batter into prepared pan. In small bowl, beat
cream cheese, remaining ½ cup sugar and remaining 1
egg until blended. Remove wrappers from 12 chocolate
pieces. Coarsely chop; stir into cream cheese mixture.
Drop batter by spoonfuls over top of chocolate mixture
in pan. Swirl with knife for marbled effect. Bake 35 to
40 minutes or just until set. Cool completely in pan on
wire rack. Cut into bars. Remove wrappers from
remaining chocolate pieces; press onto tops of bars.
Cover; refrigerate leftover bars.

Makes about 3 dozen bars

Praline Bars

¾ cup (1½ sticks) butter or margarine,
    softened
1 cup sugar, divided
1 teaspoon vanilla, divided
1½ cups flour
2 packages (8 ounces each)
    PHILADELPHIA BRAND® Cream
    Cheese, softened
2 eggs
½ cup almond brickle chips
3 tablespoons caramel ice cream topping

MIX butter, ½ cup of the sugar and ½ teaspoon of the vanilla with electric mixer on medium speed until light and fluffy. Gradually add flour, mixing on low speed until blended. Press onto bottom of 13×9-inch baking pan. Bake at 350°F for 20 to 23 minutes or until lightly browned.

MIX cream cheese, remaining ½ cup sugar and ½ teaspoon vanilla with electric mixer on medium speed until well blended. Add eggs; mix well. Blend in chips. Pour over crust. Dot top of cream cheese mixture with topping. Cut through batter with knife several times for marble effect.

BAKE at 350°F for 30 minutes. Cool in pan on wire rack. Refrigerate. Cut into bars.

Makes 2 dozen bars

Chocolate Cheesecake Bars

BROWNIES
- 1½ cups firmly packed light brown sugar
- ⅔ CRISCO® Stick or ⅔ cup CRISCO all-vegetable shortening
- 1 tablespoon water
- 1 teaspoon vanilla
- 2 eggs
- 1½ cups all-purpose flour
- ⅓ cup unsweetened cocoa powder
- ½ teaspoon salt
- ¼ teaspoon baking soda
- 2 cups (12 ounces) miniature semisweet chocolate chips

TOPPING
- 1 (8-ounce) plus 1 (3-ounce) package cream cheese, softened
- 2 eggs
- ¾ cup granulated sugar
- 1 teaspoon vanilla

1. Heat oven to 350°F. **Grease** 13×9-inch baking pan. **Place** cooling rack on countertop.

2. *For brownies,* place brown sugar, shortening, water and vanilla in large bowl. **Beat** at medium speed of electric mixer until well blended. **Add** eggs; beat well.

3. Combine flour, cocoa, salt and baking soda. **Add** to shortening mixture; beat at low speed just until blended. **Stir** in small chocolate chips. **Spread** dough evenly onto bottom of prepared pan.

4. *For topping,* place cream cheese, eggs, granulated sugar and vanilla in medium bowl. **Beat** at medium speed until well blended. **Spread** evenly over top of brownie mixture.

5. Bake at 350°F for 35 to 40 minutes or until set. *Do not overbake.* **Place** on cooling rack. **Run** spatula around edge of pan to loosen. **Cool** completely on cooling rack. **Cut** into 2×1½-inch bars. **Garnish** as desired.   *Makes about 3 dozen brownies*

Norwegian Almond Squares

1¾ cups all-purpose flour
1 cup sugar
¼ cup ground almonds
1 cup butter or margarine, softened
1 egg
1 teaspoon ground cinnamon
½ teaspoon salt
1 egg white
¾ cup sliced almonds

Preheat oven to 350°F. Beat flour, sugar, ground almonds, butter, egg, cinnamon and salt in large bowl with electric mixer at low speed 2 to 3 minutes until well mixed, scraping bowl often. Press dough onto ungreased cookie sheet to ¹⁄₁₆-inch thickness. Beat egg white with fork in small bowl until foamy. Brush over dough; sprinkle with almonds. Bake 12 to 15 minutes until very lightly browned. Immediately cut into 2-inch squares and remove from pan. Cool; store tightly covered.   *Makes 36 to 48 squares*

Chewy Toffee Almond Bars

1 cup (2 sticks) butter (do *not* use
  margarine), softened
½ cup sugar
2 cups all-purpose flour
1¾ cups (10-ounce package) SKOR®
  English Toffee Bits
¾ cup light corn syrup
1 cup sliced almonds, divided
¾ cup MOUNDS® Sweetened Coconut
  Flakes, divided

Heat oven to 350°F. Grease sides of 13×9×2-inch
baking pan. In large bowl, beat butter and sugar until
creamy. Gradually add flour, beating until well blended.
Press dough into prepared pan. Bake 15 to 20 minutes
or until edges are lightly browned. Meanwhile, in
medium saucepan, stir together toffee bits and corn
syrup. Cook over medium heat, stirring constantly,
until toffee is melted, about 12 minutes. Stir in ½ cup
almonds and ½ cup coconut. Spread toffee mixture to
within ¼ inch of edges of crust. Sprinkle remaining ½
cup almonds and remaining ¼ cup coconut over top.
Continue baking 15 minutes or until bubbly. Cool
completely in pan on wire rack. Cut into bars.

Makes about 36 bars

Caramel Marshmallow Bars

CRUMB MIXTURE
1¼ cups all-purpose flour
¼ cup graham cracker crumbs
½ cup sugar
½ cup butter or margarine, softened
¼ teaspoon salt
½ cup chopped salted peanuts

FILLING
¾ cup caramel ice cream topping
½ cup salted peanuts
½ cup miniature marshmallows
½ cup milk chocolate chips

1. Preheat oven to 350°F. Grease and flour 9-inch square baking pan.

2. For crumb mixture, beat flour, graham cracker crumbs, sugar, butter and salt in small bowl with electric mixer at low speed 1 to 2 minutes until mixture is crumbly, scraping bowl often. Stir in nuts. Reserve ¾ cup crumb mixture. Press remaining crumb mixture on bottom of prepared pan. Bake 10 to 12 minutes until lightly browned.

3. For filling, spread caramel topping evenly over hot crust. Sprinkle with nuts, marshmallows and chips. Crumble ¾ cup reserved crumb mixture over chips. Bake 10 to 12 minutes more until marshmallows just start to brown. Cool on wire rack about 30 minutes. Cover; refrigerate 1 to 2 hours or until firm. Cut into bars. Store tightly covered.   *Makes about 30 bars*

Chocolate Caramel Bars

CRUST

MAZOLA NO STICK® Corn Oil Cooking Spray

2 **cups flour**

¾ **cup (1½ sticks) MAZOLA® Margarine or butter, slightly softened**

½ **cup packed brown sugar**

¼ **teaspoon salt**

1 **cup (6 ounces) semisweet or milk chocolate chips**

CARAMEL

¾ **cup (1½ sticks) MAZOLA® Margarine or butter**

1 **cup packed brown sugar**

⅓ **cup KARO® Light or Dark Corn Syrup**

1 **teaspoon vanilla**

½ **cup chopped walnuts**

1. For Crust: Preheat oven to 350°F. Spray 13×9×2-inch baking pan with cooking spray.

2. In large bowl with mixer at medium speed, beat flour, margarine, brown sugar and salt until mixture resembles coarse crumbs; press firmly into prepared baking pan.

3. Bake 15 minutes or until golden brown. Sprinkle chocolate chips over hot crust; let stand 5 minutes or until shiny and soft. Spread chocolate evenly; set aside.

4. For Caramel: In heavy 2-quart saucepan combine margarine, brown sugar, corn syrup and vanilla. Stirring frequently, bring to boil over medium heat. Without stirring, boil 4 minutes. Pour over chocolate; spread evenly. Sprinkle with walnuts. Cool completely.

5. Refrigerate 1 hour to set chocolate; let stand at room temperature until softened. Cut into 2×1-inch bars. Store in tightly covered container at room temperature.   *Makes about 4 dozen bars*

Butterscotch Pan Cookies

- 1 **package DUNCAN HINES® Moist Deluxe French Vanilla Cake Mix**
- 2 **eggs**
- 1 **cup butter or margarine, melted**
- ¾ **cup firmly packed light brown sugar**
- 1 **teaspoon vanilla extract**
- 1 **package (12 ounces) butterscotch flavored chips**
- 1½ **cups chopped pecans**

1. Preheat oven to 375°F. Grease 15½×10½×1-inch jelly-roll pan.

2. Combine cake mix, eggs, melted butter, brown sugar and vanilla extract in large bowl. Beat at low speed with electric mixer until smooth and creamy. Stir in butterscotch chips and pecans. Spread in pan. Bake at 375°F for 20 to 25 minutes or until golden brown. Cool completely. Cut into bars.   *Makes 48 bars*

Brownie Caramel Pecan Bars

½ cup sugar
2 tablespoons butter or margarine
2 tablespoons water
2 cups (12-ounce package) HERSHEY'S
Semi-Sweet Chocolate Chips, divided
2 eggs
1 teaspoon vanilla extract
⅔ cup all-purpose flour
¼ teaspoon baking soda
¼ teaspoon salt
Caramel Topping (recipe follows)
1 cup pecan pieces

Heat oven to 350°F. Line 9-inch square baking pan with foil, extending foil over edges of pan. Grease and flour foil. In medium saucepan, combine sugar, butter and water; cook over low heat, stirring constantly, until mixture comes to a boil. Remove from heat. Immediately add 1 cup chocolate chips; stir until melted. Beat in eggs and vanilla until well blended. Stir together flour, baking soda and salt; stir into chocolate mixture. Spread into prepared pan. Bake 15 to 20 minutes or until brownies begin to pull away from sides of pan. Meanwhile, prepare Caramel Topping. Remove brownies from oven; immediately and carefully spread with prepared topping. Sprinkle remaining 1 cup chips and pecans over topping. Cool completely in pan on wire rack, being careful not to disturb chips while still soft. Use foil to lift brownies out of pan; peel off foil. Cut into bars.

Makes about 16 bars

Caramel Topping

25 caramels
¼ cup (½ stick) butter or margarine
2 tablespoons milk

Remove wrappers from caramels. In medium
microwave-safe bowl, place caramels, butter and milk.
Microwave at HIGH (100%) 1 minute; stir. Microwave
an additional 1 to 2 minutes, stirring every 30 seconds,
or until caramels are melted and mixture is smooth
when stirred. Use immediately.

Double Chocolate Crispy Bars

6 cups crispy rice cereal
½ cup peanut butter
⅓ cup butter or margarine
2 squares (1 ounce each) unsweetened chocolate
1 package (8 ounces) marshmallows
1 cup (6 ounces) semi-sweet chocolate chips *or* 6 ounces bittersweet chocolate, chopped
2 teaspoons shortening, divided
6 ounces white chocolate, chopped

1. Preheat oven to 350°F. Line 13×9-inch cookie sheet with waxed paper.

2. Spread cereal on cookie sheet; toast in oven 10 minutes or until crispy. Place in large bowl.

3. Meanwhile, combine peanut butter, butter and unsweetened chocolate in large, heavy saucepan. Stir over low heat until chocolate is melted. Add marshmallows; stir until melted and smooth. Pour peanut butter mixture over cereal; mix until evenly coated. Press into prepared pan.

4. Place semi-sweet chocolate and 1 teaspoon shortening in medium bowl. Place bowl over very warm water; stir until chocolate is melted. Spread top of bars with melted chocolate; cool until chocolate is set. Turn bars out of pan onto sheet of waxed paper, chocolate side down. Remove waxed paper from bottom of bars.

5. Melt white chocolate and remaining 1 teaspoon shortening as directed in step 4. Spread melted white chocolate over bottoms of bars. Cool until white chocolate is set. Cut into 2×1½-inch bars. Store tightly covered.   *Makes 36 bars*

Crispy Cocoa Bars

¼   **cup (½ stick) butter or margarine**
¼   **cup HERSHEY؛S Cocoa**
5   **cups miniature marshmallows**
5   **cups crisp rice cereal**

Spray 13×9×2-inch pan with vegetable cooking spray. In large saucepan over low heat, melt butter; stir in cocoa and marshmallows. Cook over low heat, stirring constantly, until marshmallows are melted and mixture is smooth and well blended. Continue cooking 1 minute, stirring constantly. Remove from heat. Add cereal; stir until coated. Lightly spray spatula with vegetable cooking spray; press mixture into prepared pan. Cool completely. Cut into bars.

Makes 24 bars

Marshmallow Krispie Bars

1 package (19.8 ounces) DUNCAN
   HINES® Chewy Fudge Brownie Mix
1 package (10½ ounces) miniature
   marshmallows
1½ cups semi-sweet chocolate chips
1 cup JIF® Creamy Peanut Butter
1 tablespoon butter or margarine
1½ cups crisp rice cereal

1. Preheat oven to 350°F. Grease bottom of 13×9-inch baking pan.

2. Prepare and bake brownies following package directions. Remove from oven. Sprinkle marshmallows on hot brownies. Return to oven. Bake for 3 minutes longer.

3. Place chocolate chips, peanut butter and butter in medium saucepan. Cook over low heat, stirring constantly, until chips are melted. Add rice cereal; mix well. Spread mixture over marshmallow layer. Refrigerate until chilled. Cut into bars.

Makes about 2 dozen bars

Tip: For a special presentation, cut cookies into diamond shapes.

The Original KELLOGG'S® Rice Krispies Treats® Recipe

3 tablespoons margarine
1 package (10 ounces) regular
    marshmallows (about 40) *or* 4 cups
    miniature marshmallows
6 cups KELLOGG'S® RICE KRISPIES®
    cereal
    Vegetable cooking spray

1. Melt margarine in large saucepan over low heat. Add marshmallows and stir until completely melted. Remove from heat.

2. Add KELLOGG'S® RICE KRISPIES® cereal. Stir until well coated.

3. Using buttered spatula or waxed paper, press mixture evenly into 13×9×2-inch pan coated with cooking spray. Cut into 2-inch squares when cool.

Makes 24 treats

Note: Use fresh marshmallows for best results. Do not use diet or reduced fat margarine.

Microwave Directions: Microwave margarine and marshmallows at HIGH 2 minutes in microwave-safe mixing bowl. Stir to combine. Microwave at HIGH 1 minute longer. Stir until smooth. Add cereal. Stir until well coated. Press into pan as directed in Step 3.

Chocolate Scotcheroos

1   cup light corn syrup
1   cup sugar
1   cup peanut butter
6   cups KELLOGG'S® RICE KRISPIES®
     cereal
     Vegetable cooking spray
1   package (6-ounce, 1 cup) semisweet
     chocolate chips
1   package (6-ounce, 1 cup) butterscotch
     chips

Combine corn syrup and sugar in large saucepan. Cook over medium heat, stirring frequently, until sugar dissolves and mixture begins to boil. Remove from heat. Stir in peanut butter; mix well. Add KELLOGG'S® RICE KRISPIES® cereal. Stir until well coated. Press mixture into 13×9-inch baking pan coated with cooking spray. Set aside.

Melt chocolate and butterscotch chips together in small saucepan over low heat, stirring constantly. Spread evenly over cereal mixture. Let stand until firm. Cut into 2×1-inch bars when cool.

Makes 4 dozen bars

Rocky Road Bars

2 cups (12-ounce package) NESTLÉ®
   TOLL HOUSE® Semi-Sweet
   Chocolate Morsels, *divided*
1½ cups all-purpose flour
1½ teaspoons baking powder
1 cup granulated sugar
6 tablespoons (¾ stick) butter or
   margarine, softened
1½ teaspoons vanilla extract
2 eggs
2 cups (4 ounces) miniature
   marshmallows
1½ cups coarsely chopped walnuts

MICROWAVE *1 cup* morsels in medium, microwave-safe bowl on HIGH (100%) power for 1 minute; stir. Microwave at additional 10- to 20-second intervals; stir until smooth. Cool to room temperature. Combine flour and baking powder in small bowl.

BEAT sugar, butter and vanilla in large mixer bowl until crumbly. Beat in eggs. Add melted chocolate; beat until smooth. Gradually beat in flour mixture. Spread batter into greased 13×9-inch baking pan.

BAKE in preheated 375°F. oven for 16 to 20 minutes or until wooden pick inserted in center comes out still slightly sticky.

REMOVE from oven; sprinkle immediately with marshmallows, nuts and *remaining* morsels. Return to oven for 2 minutes. Remove from oven; cool in pan on wire rack.   *Makes 2½ dozen bars*

Pecan Pie Bars

Bar Cookie Crust (recipe follows)
2 **eggs**
¾ **cup KARO® Light or Dark Corn Syrup**
¾ **cup sugar**
2 **tablespoons MAZOLA® Margarine or
     butter, melted**
1 **teaspoon vanilla**
1¼ **cups coarsely chopped pecans**

1. Preheat oven to 350°F. Prepare Bar Cookie Crust.

2. Meanwhile, in large bowl beat eggs, corn syrup, sugar, margarine and vanilla until well blended. Stir in pecans. Pour over hot crust; spread evenly.

3. Bake 20 minutes or until filling is firm around edges and slightly firm in center. Cool completely on wire rack. Cut into 2×1½-inch bars.

Makes about 32 bars

Bar Cookie Crust

**MAZOLA NO STICK® Corn Oil Cooking
     Spray**
2 **cups flour**
½ **cup (1 stick) cold MAZOLA® Margarine
     or butter, cut into pieces**
⅓ **cup sugar**
¼ **teaspoon salt**

1. Preheat oven to 350°F. Spray 13×9-inch baking pan with cooking spray.

2. In large bowl with mixer at medium speed, beat flour, margarine, sugar and salt until mixture resembles coarse crumbs. Press firmly into bottom and ¼ inch up sides of prepared pan.

3. Bake 15 minutes or until golden brown. Top with desired filling. Complete as recipe directs.

Chewy Rocky Road Bars

1½ cups finely crushed unsalted pretzels
¾ cup (1½ sticks) butter or margarine, melted
1 can (14 ounces) sweetened condensed milk (*not* evaporated milk)
2 cups miniature marshmallows
1 cup HERSHEY‚S Butterscotch Chips
1 cup HERSHEY‚S Semi-Sweet Chocolate Chips
1 cup MOUNDS® Sweetened Coconut Flakes
¾ cup chopped nuts

Heat oven to 350°F. In small bowl, combine pretzels and butter; spread mixture onto bottom of ungreased 13×9×2-inch baking pan. Pour sweetened condensed milk over crumb mixture, spreading to edges of pan. Top with marshmallows, butterscotch chips, chocolate chips, coconut and nuts. Press toppings firmly into sweetened condensed milk. Bake 25 to 30 minutes or until lightly browned. Cool completely in pan on wire rack. Cut into bars.   *Makes about 36 bars*

Chocolate-Topped Peanut Bars

Bar Cookie Crust (page 252)
- ½ cup packed brown sugar
- ⅓ cup KARO® Light or Dark Corn Syrup
- 2 tablespoons MAZOLA® Margarine or butter
- ¼ cup heavy or whipping cream
- 1½ cups cocktail or dry roasted peanuts
- 1 teaspoon vanilla
- ⅓ cup (2 ounces) semisweet chocolate chips

1. Preheat oven to 350°F. Prepare Bar Cookie Crust according to recipe directions.

2. In heavy 2-quart saucepan combine brown sugar, corn syrup, margarine and cream. Bring to boil; remove from heat. Stir in peanuts and vanilla. Pour over hot crust; spread evenly.

3. Bake 12 to 15 minutes or until filling is set around edges and center is slightly firm. Remove pan to wire rack.

4. Sprinkle with chocolate; let stand 5 minutes. Spread chocolate randomly with tip of knife. Cool. Refrigerate 15 minutes to set chocolate. Cut into 2×1½-inch bars.

Makes about 32 bars

Peanut Butter Chip and Walnut Squares

1 cup (2 sticks) butter or margarine, softened
1 cup packed light brown sugar
1 egg
1 teaspoon vanilla extract
2 cups all-purpose flour
½ cup light corn syrup
6 tablespoons butter or margarine
1⅔ cups (10-ounce package) REESE'S® Peanut Butter Chips
¾ cup chopped walnuts

Heat oven to 350°F. In large bowl, beat 1 cup butter, brown sugar, egg and vanilla until light and fluffy. Stir in flour. Spread batter into ungreased 13×9×2-inch baking pan. Bake 20 to 22 minutes or until lightly browned. Cool completely in pan on wire rack. In medium saucepan over low heat, cook corn syrup, 6 tablespoons butter and peanut butter chips, stirring constantly until chips are melted. Working quickly, spread mixture over baked layer. Sprinkle with walnuts; gently press into mixture. Refrigerate, uncovered, about 2 hours or until firm. Cut into squares. *Makes about 36 squares*

Spiced Chocolate Pecan Squares

COOKIE BASE
- 1 cup all-purpose flour
- ½ cup packed light brown sugar
- ½ teaspoon baking soda
- ¼ cup (½ stick) butter or margarine, softened

TOPPING
- 1 package (8 ounces) semi-sweet chocolate baking squares
- 2 large eggs
- ¼ cup packed light brown sugar
- ¼ cup light corn syrup
- 2 tablespoons FRENCH'S® Worcestershire Sauce
- 1 tablespoon vanilla extract
- 1½ cups chopped pecans or walnuts, divided

Preheat oven to 375°F. To prepare cookie base, place flour, ½ cup sugar and baking soda in food processor or bowl of electric mixer. Process or mix 10 seconds. Add butter. Process or beat 30 seconds or until mixture resembles fine crumbs. Press evenly into bottom of greased 9-inch baking pan. Bake 15 minutes.

Meanwhile, to prepare topping, place chocolate in microwave-safe bowl. Microwave, uncovered, on HIGH 2 minutes or until chocolate is melted, stirring until chocolate is smooth; set aside.

Place eggs, ¼ cup sugar, corn syrup, Worcestershire and vanilla in food processor or bowl of electric mixer. Process or beat until well blended. Add melted chocolate. Process or beat until smooth. Stir in *1 cup* nuts. Pour chocolate mixture over cookie base. Sprinkle with remaining *½ cup* nuts. Bake 40 minutes or until toothpick inserted into center comes out with slightly fudgy crumbs. (Cookie will be slightly puffed along edges.) Cool completely on wire rack. To serve, cut into squares. *Makes 16 squares*

Chocolate Chip Walnut Bars

Bar Cookie Crust (page 252)
2 eggs
½ cup KARO® Light or Dark Corn Syrup
½ cup sugar
2 tablespoons MAZOLA® Margarine or
      butter, melted
1 cup (6 ounces) semisweet chocolate
      chips
¾ cup chopped walnuts

1. Preheat oven to 350°F. Prepare Bar Cookie Crust.

2. Meanwhile, in medium bowl beat eggs, corn syrup, sugar and margarine until well blended. Stir in chocolate chips and walnuts. Pour over hot crust; spread evenly.

3. Bake 15 to 18 minutes or until set. Cool completely on wire rack. Cut into 2×1½-inch bars.

Makes about 32 bars

Championship Chocolate Chip Bars

1½   cups all-purpose flour
½   cup packed light brown sugar
½   cup (1 stick) cold butter or margarine
2   cups (12-ounce package) HERSHEY'S
      Semi-Sweet Chocolate Chips, divided
1   can (14 ounces) sweetened condensed
      milk (*not* evaporated milk)
1   egg
1   teaspoon vanilla extract
1   cup chopped nuts

Heat oven to 350°F. In medium bowl, stir together
flour and brown sugar; with pastry blender, cut in
butter until mixture resembles coarse crumbs. Stir in
½ cup chocolate chips; press mixture onto bottom of
13×9×2-inch baking pan. Bake 15 minutes.
Meanwhile, in large bowl, combine sweetened
condensed milk, egg and vanilla. Stir in remaining 1½
cups chips and nuts. Spread over baked crust.
Continue baking 25 minutes or until golden brown.
Cool completely in pan on wire rack. Cut into bars.

Makes about 36 bars

Chocolate Amaretto Squares

½ cup (1 stick) butter (do *not* use
       margarine), melted
1 cup sugar
2 eggs
½ cup all-purpose flour
⅓ cup HERSHEY₅S Cocoa or
       HERSHEY₅S European Style Cocoa
1¼ cups ground almonds
2 tablespoons almond-flavored liqueur *or*
       ½ teaspoon almond extract
   Sliced almonds (optional)

Heat oven to 325°F. Grease 8-inch square baking pan.
In large bowl, beat butter and sugar until creamy. Add
eggs, flour and cocoa; beat well. Stir in ground
almonds and almond liqueur. Pour batter into prepared
pan. Bake 35 to 40 minutes or just until set. Cool
completely in pan on wire rack. Cut into squares.
Garnish with sliced almonds, if desired.

Makes about 16 squares

Fudgy Chocolate Mint Oatmeal Squares

1¼ cups all-purpose flour
½ teaspoon baking soda
1 cup packed brown sugar
½ cup (1 stick) butter or margarine, softened
1 egg
1½ cups quick or old-fashioned oats
1 cup chopped nuts
1½ cups (10-ounce package) NESTLÉ® TOLL HOUSE® Mint-Chocolate Morsels
1¼ cups (14-ounce can) CARNATION® Sweetened Condensed Milk
2 tablespoons butter or margarine

COMBINE flour and baking soda in small bowl. Beat sugar and ½ cup butter in large mixer bowl until creamy. Beat in egg. Gradually beat in flour mixture. Stir in oats and nuts. Press 2 cups oat mixture onto bottom of greased 13×9-inch baking pan with moistened fingers.

MELT morsels, sweetened condensed milk and 2 tablespoons butter in heavy-duty saucepan over low heat, stirring constantly until smooth; pour over crust. Crumble remaining oat mixture over filling.

BAKE in preheated 350°F. oven for 25 to 30 minutes or until filling is set and topping begins to brown. Cool in pan on wire rack.   Makes about 2½ dozen squares

OREO® Shazam Bars

28 OREO® Chocolate Sandwich Cookies
¼ cup margarine, melted
1 cup shredded coconut
1 cup white chocolate chips
½ cup chopped nuts
1 (14-ounce) can sweetened condensed milk

Finely roll 20 cookies. Mix cookie crumbs and margarine; spread over bottom of 9×9×2-inch baking pan, pressing lightly. Chop remaining cookies. Layer coconut, chips, nuts and chopped cookies in prepared pan; drizzle evenly with condensed milk. Bake at 350°F for 25 to 30 minutes or until golden and set. Cool completely. Cut into bars.   *Makes 24 bars*

KAHLÚA® Pumpkin Squares with Praline Topping

1   cup all-purpose flour
¼   cup powdered sugar
½   cup cold unsalted butter
1   cup canned solid-pack pumpkin
1   (8-ounce) package cream cheese, cut up
      and softened
2   eggs
¼   cup granulated sugar
¼   cup KAHLÚA®
1   cup chopped walnuts or pecans
¾   cup firmly packed brown sugar
¼   cup unsalted butter, melted

Preheat oven to 350°F. In medium bowl, combine flour
and powdered sugar. Using 2 knives or pastry blender,
cut in ½ cup butter until mixture forms fine crumbs.
Press mixture into bottom of 8-inch square baking
dish. Bake 15 to 18 minutes or until golden.

Meanwhile, in food processor or blender, purée
pumpkin, cream cheese, eggs, granulated sugar and
KAHLÚA® until smooth. Pour pumpkin mixture over
warm baked crust; return to oven and bake about 20
minutes or until set. Cool in dish on wire rack. Cover;
refrigerate.

In small bowl, combine nuts, brown sugar and melted
butter. Just before serving, sprinkle nut mixture over
pumpkin filling.   *Makes about 16 squares*

Pumpkin Harvest Bars

1¾ cups all-purpose flour
2 teaspoons baking powder
1 teaspoon grated orange peel
1 teaspoon ground cinnamon
½ teaspoon salt
½ teaspoon ground nutmeg
¼ teaspoon ground ginger
¼ teaspoon ground cloves
¾ cup sugar
½ cup MOTT'S® Natural Apple Sauce
½ cup solid-pack pumpkin
1 whole egg
1 egg white
2 tablespoons vegetable oil
½ cup raisins

1. Preheat oven to 350°F. Spray 13×9-inch baking pan with nonstick cooking spray.

2. In small bowl, combine flour, baking powder, orange peel, cinnamon, salt, nutmeg, ginger and cloves.

3. In large bowl, combine sugar, apple sauce, pumpkin, whole egg, egg white and oil.

4. Add flour mixture to apple sauce mixture; stir until well blended. Stir in raisins. Spread batter into prepared pan.

5. Bake 25 to 30 minutes or until toothpick inserted in center comes out clean. Cool on wire rack 15 minutes; cut into 16 bars. *Makes 16 bars*

Tropical Sun Bars

CRUST

 1 **cup all-purpose flour**
 ¼ **cup sugar**
 ⅓ **cup margarine, softened**
 1 **tablespoon grated tangerine or orange peel**

FILLING

 ½ **cup sugar**
 ½ **cup flaked coconut**
 2 **tablespoons all-purpose flour**
 ½ **teaspoon baking powder**
 ⅛ **teaspoon salt**
 1½ **tablespoons grated tangerine or orange peel**
 2 **eggs**
 1 **tablespoon orange juice**
 1 **tablespoon orange liqueur**
 Thin strips of orange peel (optional)

1. Preheat oven to 350°F.

2. For crust, beat 1 cup flour, ¼ cup sugar, margarine and 1 tablespoon tangerine peel in small bowl with electric mixer at low speed 1 to 2 minutes until coarse crumbs form, scraping bowl often. Press on bottom of 9-inch square baking pan.

3. Bake 10 to 12 minutes until edges are lightly browned.

4. For filling, beat ½ cup sugar, coconut, 2 tablespoons flour, baking powder, salt, 1½ tablespoons tangerine peel, eggs, orange juice and liqueur in small bowl at medium speed 1 to 2 minutes until well blended, scraping bowl often. Pour over hot crust.

5. Bake 20 to 25 minutes more until edges are lightly browned. Immediately sprinkle with orange peel, if desired. Cool completely. Cut into bars. Store tightly covered.   *Makes about 24 bars*

 Blockbuster

BROWNIES

Chewy Chocolate Brownies

¾ cup granulated sugar
½ cup (1 stick) butter or margarine
2 tablespoons water
4 bars (2 ounces *each*) NESTLÉ® TOLL HOUSE® Semi-Sweet Baking Chocolate, broken into pieces
2 eggs
2 teaspoons vanilla extract
1 cup all-purpose flour
¼ teaspoon baking soda
¼ teaspoon salt
½ cup chopped nuts (optional)

MICROWAVE sugar, butter and water in large, microwave-safe bowl on HIGH (100%) power for 3 minutes or until mixture boils, stirring once. Add baking bars; stir until melted.

STIR in eggs one at a time until well blended. Stir in vanilla. Add flour, baking soda and salt; stir well. Stir in nuts. Pour into greased 13×9-inch baking pan.

BAKE in preheated 350°F. oven for 16 to 20 minutes or until wooden pick inserted in center comes out still slightly sticky. Cool in pan.

Makes about 2 dozen brownies

For Saucepan Method: BRING sugar, butter and water in medium saucepan just to a boil, stirring constantly. Remove from heat. Proceed as above.

Chocolate Syrup Brownies

- 1 egg
- 1 cup packed light brown sugar
- ¾ cup HERSHEY'S Syrup
- 1½ cups all-purpose flour
- ¼ teaspoon baking soda
  Dash salt
- ½ cup (1 stick) butter (do *not* use margarine), melted
- ¾ cup chopped pecans or walnuts

Heat oven to 350°F. Grease 9-inch square baking pan. In small bowl, beat egg lightly; add brown sugar and syrup, beating until well blended. Stir together flour, baking soda and salt; gradually add to egg mixture, beating until blended. Stir in butter and nuts. Spread batter into prepared pan. Bake 35 to 40 minutes or until brownies begin to pull away from sides of pan. Cool completely in pan on wire rack. Cut into squares.

Makes about 16 brownies

Outrageous Brownies

½ cup MIRACLE WHIP® Salad Dressing
2 eggs, beaten
¼ cup cold water
1 (21.5-ounce) package fudge brownie
   mix
3 (7-ounce) milk chocolate bars, divided
   Walnut halves (optional)

PREHEAT oven to 350°F.

MIX together salad dressing, eggs and water until well blended. Stir in brownie mix, mixing just until moistened.

COARSELY chop 2 chocolate bars; stir into brownie mixture. Pour into greased 13×9-inch baking pan.

BAKE 30 to 35 minutes or until edges begin to pull away from sides of pan. Immediately top with 1 chopped chocolate bar. Let stand about 5 minutes or until melted; spread evenly over brownies. Garnish with walnut halves, if desired. Cool. Cut into squares.

Makes about 24 brownies

Bittersweet Brownies

MAZOLA NO STICK® Cooking Spray
4 squares (1 ounce each) unsweetened
   chocolate, melted
1 cup sugar
½ cup HELLMANN'S® or BEST FOODS®
   Real or Light Mayonnaise
2 eggs
1 teaspoon vanilla
¾ cup flour
½ teaspoon baking powder
¼ teaspoon salt
½ cup chopped walnuts

1. Preheat oven to 350°F. Spray 8×8×2-inch baking pan with cooking spray.

2. In large bowl, stir chocolate, sugar, mayonnaise, eggs and vanilla until smooth. Stir in flour, baking powder and salt until well blended. Stir in walnuts. Spread evenly in prepared pan.

3. Bake 25 to 30 minutes or until wooden pick inserted into center comes out clean. Cool in pan on wire rack. Cut into 2-inch squares.   *Makes 16 brownies*

Easy Double Chocolate Chip Brownies

   2   cups (12-ounce package) NESTLÉ®
         TOLL HOUSE® Semi-Sweet
         Chocolate Morsels, *divided*
   ½   cup (1 stick) butter or margarine, cut
         into pieces
   3   eggs
  1¼ cups all-purpose flour
   1   cup granulated sugar
   1   teaspoon vanilla extract
   ¼   teaspoon baking soda
   ½   cup chopped nuts

MELT *1 cup* morsels and butter in large, heavy-duty saucepan over low heat, stirring until smooth. Remove from heat. Add eggs; stir well. Add flour, sugar, vanilla and baking soda; stir well. Stir in *remaining 1 cup* morsels and nuts. Spread into greased 13×9-inch baking pan.

BAKE in preheated 350°F. oven for 18 to 22 minutes or until wooden pick inserted in center comes out slightly sticky. Cool completely in pan on wire rack.

Makes 2 dozen brownies

Best Brownies

½ **cup (1 stick) butter or margarine,
   melted**
1 **cup sugar**
1 **teaspoon vanilla extract**
2 **eggs**
½ **cup all-purpose flour**
⅓ **cup HERSHEY®S Cocoa**
¼ **teaspoon baking powder**
¼ **teaspoon salt**
½ **cup chopped nuts (optional)**
   **Creamy Brownie Frosting (recipe
   follows)**

Heat oven to 350°F. Grease 9-inch square baking pan.
In medium bowl, stir together butter, sugar and
vanilla. Add eggs; with spoon, beat well. Stir together
flour, cocoa, baking powder and salt. Add to egg
mixture; beat until well blended. Stir in nuts, if
desired. Spread batter into prepared pan. Bake 20 to 25
minutes or until brownies begin to pull away from
sides of pan. Cool completely in pan on wire rack.
Prepare Creamy Brownie Frosting; spread over
brownies. Cut into squares.

Makes about 16 brownies

Creamy Brownie Frosting

3 tablespoons butter or margarine,
   softened
3 tablespoons HERSHEY®S Cocoa
1 tablespoon light corn syrup or honey
½ teaspoon vanilla extract
1 cup powdered sugar
1 tablespoon milk

In small bowl, beat butter, cocoa, corn syrup and
vanilla until blended. Add powdered sugar and milk;
beat until smooth and of spreading consistency. Add
additional milk, ½ teaspoon at a time, if needed.

Chocolate Brownies Deluxe

½ cup (1 stick) butter or margarine,
   softened
1 cup sugar
2 eggs
1 teaspoon vanilla extract
1¼ cups all-purpose flour
¼ cup HERSHEY'S Cocoa
¼ teaspoon baking soda
¾ cup HERSHEY'S Syrup
1 cup REESE'S Peanut Butter Chips
   (optional)
   Fudge Brownie Frosting (recipe
   follows)

Heat oven to 350°F. Grease 13×9×2-inch baking pan.
In large bowl, beat butter, sugar, eggs and vanilla until
light and fluffy. Stir together flour, cocoa and baking
soda; add alternately with syrup to butter mixture,
beating well after each addition. Stir in peanut butter
chips, if desired. Spread batter into prepared pan. Bake
40 to 45 minutes or until brownies begin to pull away
from sides of pan. Cool completely in pan on wire rack.
Prepare Fudge Brownie Frosting; spread over
brownies. Cut into bars.   *Makes about 24 brownies*

Fudge Brownie Frosting

3   **tablespoons butter or margarine, softened**
3   **tablespoons HERSHEY®S Cocoa**
1   **cup powdered sugar**
1   **tablespoon milk**
¾   **teaspoon vanilla extract**

In small bowl, beat butter and cocoa until well blended; gradually add powdered sugar alternately with combined milk and vanilla, beating until smooth and of spreading consistency. Add additional milk, ½ teaspoon at a time, if needed.

Double "Topped" Brownies

BROWNIES
1 package DUNCAN HINES® Double Fudge Brownie Mix
2 eggs
⅓ cup water
¼ cup CRISCO® Oil or CRISCO® PURITAN® Canola Oil
½ cup flaked coconut
½ cup chopped nuts

FROSTING
3 cups confectioners sugar
⅓ cup butter or margarine, softened
1½ teaspoons vanilla extract
2 to 3 tablespoons milk

TOPPING
3 squares (3 ounces) unsweetened chocolate
1 tablespoon butter or margarine

1. Preheat oven to 350°F. Grease bottom of 13×9×2-inch pan.

2. For brownies, combine brownie mix, fudge packet from Mix, eggs, water and oil in large bowl. Stir with spoon until well blended, about 50 strokes. Stir in coconut and nuts. Spread in pan. Bake at 350°F for 27 to 30 minutes or until set. Cool completely.

3. For frosting, combine confectioners sugar, ⅓ cup butter and vanilla extract. Stir in milk, 1 tablespoon at a time, until frosting is spreading consistency. Spread over brownies. Refrigerate until frosting is firm, about 30 minutes.

4. For topping, melt chocolate and 1 tablespoon butter in small bowl over hot water; stir until smooth. Drizzle over frosting. Refrigerate until chocolate is firm, about 15 minutes. Cut into bars.

Makes about 48 brownies

Tip: Chocolate topping can be prepared in microwave oven. Place chocolate and butter in microwave-safe bowl and microwave at MEDIUM (50% power) for 2 to 2½ minutes; stir until smooth.

Orange Cappuccino Brownies

¾ cup butter
2 squares (1 ounce each) semisweet chocolate, coarsely chopped
2 squares (1 ounce each) unsweetened chocolate, coarsely chopped
1¾ cups granulated sugar
1 tablespoon instant coffee granules
3 eggs
¼ cup orange-flavored liqueur
2 teaspoons grated orange peel
1 cup all-purpose flour
1 package (12 ounces) semisweet chocolate chips
2 tablespoons vegetable shortening

1. Preheat oven to 350°F. Grease 13×9-inch baking pan.

2. Melt butter and chopped chocolates in large, heavy saucepan over low heat, stirring constantly. Stir in granulated sugar and coffee granules. Remove from heat. Cool slightly.

3. Beat in eggs, 1 at a time, with wire whisk. Whisk in liqueur and orange peel. Beat flour into chocolate mixture until just blended. Spread batter evenly in prepared pan.

4. Bake 25 to 30 minutes until center is just set. Remove pan to wire rack. Meanwhile, melt chocolate chips and shortening in small, heavy saucepan over low heat, stirring constantly. Immediately, spread hot chocolate mixture over warm brownies. Cool completely in pan on wire rack. Cut into 2-inch squares. Store tightly covered.

Makes about 2 dozen brownies

Frosted Maraschino Brownies

- 24 **red maraschino cherries, drained**
- 1 **package (23.6 ounces) brownie mix, plus ingredients to prepare mix**
- 2 **cups powdered sugar**
- ½ **cup plus 1 tablespoon butter or margarine, softened, divided**
- 3 **tablespoons milk**
- 2 **tablespoons instant vanilla pudding mix**
- 1 **ounce sweet baking chocolate**

Preheat oven to temperature directed on brownie mix. Pat cherries with paper towel to remove excess juice; set aside. Prepare and bake brownie mix according to package directions in 13×9-inch baking pan; cool completely in pan on wire rack.

For frosting, beat sugar, ½ cup butter, milk and pudding mix in medium bowl until smooth. Cover; refrigerate until slightly thickened. Spread over cooled brownie in pan. Arrange cherries in rows over frosting. In small saucepan, over low heat, melt chocolate and remaining 1 tablespoon butter; stir to blend. Cool slightly. Drizzle chocolate mixture over frosting. Let chocolate set before cutting.

Makes about 24 brownies

Favorite recipe from **National Cherry Foundation**

Chocolate Espresso Brownies

4 squares (1 ounce each) unsweetened
   chocolate
1 cup granulated sugar
¼ cup Prune Purée (recipe follows)
3 egg whites
1 to 2 tablespoons instant espresso coffee
   powder
1 teaspoon baking powder
1 teaspoon salt
1 teaspoon vanilla
½ cup all-purpose flour
   Powdered sugar (optional)

Preheat oven to 350°F. Coat 8-inch square baking pan
with vegetable cooking spray. In small heavy saucepan,
melt chocolate over very low heat, stirring until melted
and smooth. Remove from heat; cool. In mixer bowl,
beat chocolate and remaining ingredients except flour
and powdered sugar at medium speed until well
blended; mix in flour. Spread batter evenly in prepared
pan. Bake about 30 minutes until pick inserted into
center comes out clean. Cool completely in pan on
wire rack. Dust with powdered sugar. Cut into 1⅓-inch
squares. *Makes 36 brownies*

Prune Purée: Combine 1⅓ cups (8 ounces) pitted
prunes and 6 tablespoons hot water in container of
food processor or blender. Pulse on and off until
prunes are finely chopped and smooth. Store leftovers
in a covered container in the refrigerator for up to two
months. Makes 1 cup.

Favorite recipe from **California Prune Board**

Black Russian Brownies

- **4** squares (1 ounce each) unsweetened chocolate
- **1** cup butter
- **¾** teaspoon ground black pepper
- **4** eggs, lightly beaten
- **1½** cups sugar
- **1½** teaspoons vanilla
- **⅓** cup KAHLÚA®
- **2** tablespoons vodka
- **1⅓** cups all-purpose flour
- **½** teaspoon salt
- **¼** teaspoon baking powder
- **1** cup chopped walnuts or toasted sliced almonds
- Powdered sugar (optional)

Line bottom of 13×9-inch baking pan with waxed paper. Melt chocolate and butter with black pepper in small saucepan over low heat. Remove from heat.

Combine eggs, sugar and vanilla in large bowl; beat well. Stir in cooled chocolate mixture, KAHLÚA® and vodka. Combine flour, salt and baking powder; add to chocolate mixture and stir until blended. Add walnuts. Spread in prepared pan.

Bake in 350°F oven just until toothpick inserted into center comes out clean, about 25 minutes. *Do not overbake.* Cool in pan on wire rack. Cut into bars. Sprinkle with powdered sugar, if desired.

Makes about 30 brownies

Coconut Crowned Cappuccino Brownies

6 squares (1 ounce each) semisweet chocolate, coarsely chopped
1 tablespoon freeze dried coffee granules
1 tablespoon boiling water
½ cup sugar
¼ cup butter or margarine, softened
3 eggs
¾ cup all-purpose flour
½ teaspoon baking powder
¾ teaspoon ground cinnamon
¼ teaspoon salt
¼ cup whipping cream
1 teaspoon vanilla extract
¾ cup flaked coconut, divided
½ cup semisweet chocolate chips

1. Preheat oven to 350°F. Grease 8-inch square baking pan.

2. Melt chocolate squares in small, heavy saucepan over low heat, stirring constantly. Dissolve coffee granules in boiling water in small cup. Beat sugar and butter in large bowl with electric mixer at medium speed until light and fluffy. Beat in 2 eggs, 1 at a time. Beat in chocolate and coffee mixtures until well blended. Combine flour, baking powder, cinnamon and salt in small bowl; add to butter mixture. Beat until well blended. Spread evenly in prepared pan.

3. Combine whipping cream, remaining 1 egg and vanilla in medium bowl; blend well. Stir in ½ cup coconut and chips. Spread evenly over brownie batter; sprinkle with remaining ¼ cup coconut.

4. Bake 30 to 35 minutes until coconut is browned and center is set. Remove pan to wire rack; cool completely. Cut into 2-inch squares. Store tightly covered.

Makes about 16 brownies

KAHLÚA® Mudslide Brownies

- 2 **cups all-purpose flour**
- ½ **teaspoon baking powder**
- ½ **teaspoon salt**
- ⅔ **cup butter**
- 4 **squares (1 ounce each) unsweetened chocolate, chopped**
- 3 **eggs**
- 1½ **cups granulated sugar**
- 4 **tablespoons KAHLÚA®**
- 2 **tablespoons Irish cream liqueur**
- 1 **tablespoon vodka**
- ¾ **cup coarsely chopped walnuts (optional)**
  KAHLÚA® Glaze (recipe follows)
  Whole coffee beans (optional)

Combine flour, baking powder and salt in small bowl. Melt butter and chocolate in small saucepan over low heat; set aside. Beat eggs and granulated sugar in large bowl until light and fluffy. Beat in flour mixture, chocolate mixture, 4 tablespoons KAHLÚA®, Irish cream and vodka. Fold in walnuts, if desired. Pour into greased 13×9-inch baking pan. Bake in 350°F oven just until toothpick inserted in center comes out clean, about 25 minutes. *Do not overbake.* Cool in pan on wire rack. Prepare KAHLÚA® Glaze; spread with glaze. Decorate with whole coffee beans, if desired. Cut into squares.   *Makes 24 brownies*

KAHLÚA® Glaze: Beat together 1¼ cups powdered sugar and 3 tablespoons KAHLÚA® in small bowl until smooth.

Coconut Brownie Bites

42 **MOUNDS® or ALMOND JOY® Candy Bar Miniatures**
½ **cup (1 stick) butter or margarine, softened**
½ **cup packed light brown sugar**
¼ **cup granulated sugar**
1 **egg**
1 **teaspoon vanilla extract**
1¼ **cups all-purpose flour**
⅓ **cup HERSHEY'S Cocoa**
¾ **teaspoon baking soda**
½ **teaspoon salt**

Remove wrappers from candies. Line small muffin cups (1¾ inches in diameter) with paper bake cups. In large bowl, beat butter, brown sugar, granulated sugar, egg and vanilla until light and fluffy. Stir together flour, cocoa, baking soda and salt; gradually add to butter mixture, beating until well blended. Cover; refrigerate dough about 30 minutes or until firm enough to handle. Heat oven to 375°F. Shape dough into 1-inch balls; place one in each prepared muffin cup. *Do not flatten.* Bake 8 to 10 minutes or until puffed. Remove from oven. Cool 5 minutes. (Cookie will sink slightly.) Press one candy onto each cookie. Cool completely in pan on wire racks.   *Makes about 3½ dozen cookies*

Scrumptious Minted Brownies

1 **package (19.8 ounces) DUNCAN HINES® Chewy Fudge Brownie Mix**
1 **egg**
⅓ **cup water**
⅓ **cup CRISCO® Oil or CRISCO® PURITAN® Canola Oil**
48 **chocolate crème de menthe candy wafers, divided**

1. Preheat oven to 350°F. Grease bottom of 13×9×2-inch pan.

2. Combine brownie mix, egg, water and oil in large bowl. Stir with spoon until well blended, about 50 strokes. Spread in pan.

3. Bake at 350°F for 25 minutes or until set. Place 30 candy wafers evenly over hot brownies. Let stand for 1 minute to melt. Spread candy wafers to frost brownies. Score frosting into 36 bars by running tip of knife through melted candy. (Do not cut through brownies.) Cut remaining 18 candy wafers in half lengthwise; place halves on each scored bar. Cool completely. Cut into squares. *Makes 36 brownies*

Sensational Peppermint Pattie Brownies

24 small (1½-inch) YORK® Peppermint
    Patties
1½ cups (3 sticks) butter or margarine,
    melted
3 cups sugar
1 tablespoon vanilla extract
5 eggs
2 cups all-purpose flour
1 cup HERSHEY'S Cocoa
1 teaspoon baking powder
1 teaspoon salt

Heat oven to 350°F. Remove wrappers from
peppermint patties. Grease 13×9×2-inch baking pan.
In large bowl with spoon or whisk, stir together butter,
sugar and vanilla. Add eggs; stir until well blended. Stir
together flour, cocoa, baking powder and salt;
gradually add to butter mixture, blending well. Reserve
2 cups batter. Spread remaining batter into prepared
pan. Arrange peppermint patties about ½ inch apart in
single layer over batter. Spread reserved batter over
patties. Bake 50 to 55 minutes or until brownies begin
to pull away from sides of pan. Cool completely in pan
on wire rack. Cut into squares.

Makes about 36 brownies

Minted Chocolate Chip Brownies

¾ cup granulated sugar
½ cup butter or margarine
2 tablespoons water
1 cup semisweet chocolate chips or mini
    semisweet chocolate chips
1½ teaspoons vanilla extract
2 eggs
1¼ cups all-purpose flour
½ teaspoon baking soda
½ teaspoon salt
1 cup mint chocolate chips
    Powdered sugar (optional)

1. Preheat oven to 350°F. Grease 9-inch square baking pan.

2. Combine sugar, butter and water in large microwavable bowl. Microwave on HIGH 2½ to 3 minutes or until butter is melted. Stir in semisweet chips; stir gently until chips are melted and mixture is well blended. Stir in vanilla; let stand 5 minutes to cool.

3. Beat eggs into chocolate mixture, 1 at a time. Combine flour, baking soda and salt in small bowl; add to chocolate mixture. Stir in mint chocolate chips. Spread into prepared pan.

4. Bake 25 minutes for fudgy brownies or 30 minutes for cakelike brownies. Remove pan to wire rack; cool completely. Cut into 2¼-inch squares. Sprinkle with powdered sugar, if desired. Store tightly covered.

Makes about 16 brownies

Peanut Butter Chip Brownies

½ cup butter or margarine
4 squares (1 ounce each) semisweet
     chocolate
½ cup sugar
2 eggs
1 teaspoon vanilla extract
½ cup all-purpose flour
1 package (12 ounces) peanut butter
     chips
1 cup (6 ounces) milk chocolate chips

1. Preheat oven to 350°F. Grease 8-inch square baking pan.

2. Melt butter and semisweet chocolate in small, heavy saucepan over low heat, stirring just until chocolate melts. Remove from heat; cool. Beat sugar and eggs in large bowl until light and fluffy. Blend in vanilla and chocolate mixture. Stir in flour until blended; fold in peanut butter chips. Spread evenly in prepared pan.

3. Bake 25 to 30 minutes just until firm and dry in center. Remove from oven; sprinkle milk chocolate chips over top. Place pan on wire rack. When chocolate chips have melted, spread over brownies. Refrigerate until chocolate topping is set. Cut into 2-inch squares. Store tightly covered.   *Makes 16 brownies*

Brownies with Peanut Butter Chips

1¼ cups (2½ sticks) butter or margarine, melted

1¾ cups sugar

4 eggs

2 teaspoons vanilla extract

1⅔ cups all-purpose flour

⅔ cup HERSHEY'S Cocoa

½ teaspoon baking powder

½ teaspoon salt

1⅔ cups (10-ounce package) REESE'S® Peanut Butter Chips, divided

Peanut Butter Chip Glaze (recipe follows)

Heat oven to 350°F. Grease 13×9×2-inch baking pan. In large bowl, stir together butter and sugar. Add eggs and vanilla; beat with spoon or whisk until well blended. Stir together flour, cocoa, baking powder and salt; gradually add to butter mixture, stirring until well blended. Reserve ½ cup peanut butter chips for glaze; stir remaining chips into batter. Spread batter into prepared pan. Bake 30 to 35 minutes or until wooden pick inserted in center comes out clean. Cool completely in pan on wire rack. Prepare Peanut Butter Chip Glaze; drizzle over brownies. Let stand until glaze is set. Cut into squares.

Makes about 32 brownies

Peanut Butter Chip Glaze

½ cup REESE'S® Peanut Butter Chips
    (reserved from brownies)
2 tablespoons butter or margarine
2 tablespoons milk
¼ cup powdered sugar

In small microwave-safe bowl, place peanut butter
chips, butter and milk. Microwave at HIGH (100%)
45 seconds; stir. If necessary, microwave at HIGH an
additional 15 seconds at a time, stirring after each
heating, just until chips are melted when stirred. Add
powdered sugar; beat with whisk until smooth.

Brownie Candy Cups

- 1 **package DUNCAN HINES® Double Fudge Brownie Mix**
- 2 **eggs**
- ⅓ **cup water**
- ¼ **cup CRISCO® Oil or CRISCO® PURITAN® Canola Oil**
- 30 **miniature peanut butter cup candies, wrappers removed**

1. Preheat oven to 350°F. Place 30 (2-inch) foil liners in muffin pans or on baking sheets.

2. Combine brownie mix, fudge packet from Mix, eggs, water and oil in large bowl. Stir with spoon until well blended, about 50 strokes. Place 2 level measuring tablespoons batter in each foil liner.

3. Bake at 350°F for 10 minutes. Remove from oven. Push 1 peanut butter cup candy in center of each cupcake until even with surface of brownie. Bake 5 to 7 minutes longer. Remove to cooling racks. Cool completely.   *Makes 30 brownie cups*

Mississippi Mud Brownies

1   package (19.8 ounces) DUNCAN
        HINES® Chewy Fudge Brownie Mix
2   eggs
⅓   cup water
⅓   cup CRISCO® Oil or CRISCO®
        PURITAN® Canola Oil
1   jar (7 ounces) marshmallow creme
1   container (16 ounces) DUNCAN
        HINES® Creamy Homestyle Milk
        Chocolate Frosting, melted

1. Preheat oven to 350°F. Grease bottom of 13×9-inch baking pan.

2. Combine brownie mix, eggs, water and oil in large bowl. Stir with spoon until well blended, about 50 strokes. Spread in pan. Bake at 350°F for 25 to 28 minutes or until set.

3. Spread marshmallow creme gently over hot brownies. Pour 1¼ cups melted milk chocolate frosting over marshmallow cream. Swirl with knife to marble. Cool completely. Cut into bars.

Makes 20 to 24 brownies

Note: Store leftover melted frosting in original container. Refrigerate.

Tip: For ease in spreading marshmallow creme, place spoonfuls evenly over brownie surface. Allow heat of brownies to soften marshmallow creme before spreading.

Rich Chocolate Caramel Brownies

    1   **package (18.25 to 18.5 ounces) devil's food or chocolate cake mix**
    1   **cup chopped nuts**
    ½   **cup (1 stick) butter or margarine, melted**
    1   **cup CARNATION® Evaporated Milk, *divided***
  35   **(10 ounces) light caramels, unwrapped**
    1   **cup (6 ounces) NESTLÉ® TOLL HOUSE® Semi-Sweet Chocolate Morsels**

COMBINE cake mix and nuts in large bowl; stir in butter. Stir in ⅔ *cup* evaporated milk (batter will be thick). Spread *half* of batter into greased 13×9-inch baking pan.

BAKE in preheated 350°F. oven for 15 minutes.

COMBINE caramels and *remaining* evaporated milk in small saucepan; cook over low heat until caramels are melted. Sprinkle morsels over baked layer; drizzle caramel mixture over top. Drop *remaining* batter by heaping teaspoon over caramel mixture. Bake at 350°F. for 20 to 25 minutes (top layer will be soft). Cool completely in pan on wire rack.

Makes 48 brownies

All American HEATH® Brownies

⅓ cup butter or margarine
1 square (1 ounce) unsweetened
  chocolate
1 cup sugar
2 eggs
1 teaspoon vanilla
1 cup all-purpose flour
½ teaspoon baking powder
¼ teaspoon salt
1 package (6 ounces) original HEATH®
  Bits, coarsely crushed

Preheat oven to 350°F. Grease bottom of 8-inch square baking pan.

In 1½-quart saucepan, over low heat, melt butter and chocolate, stirring occasionally. Blend in sugar. Add eggs, 1 at a time, beating after each addition. Blend in vanilla. In small bowl, combine flour, baking powder and salt; add to chocolate mixture and blend. Spread batter in prepared pan.

Bake 20 minutes or until brownie starts to pull away from edge of pan. Remove from oven; sprinkle with HEATH® Bits. Cover tightly with foil and cool completely on wire rack. Remove foil; cut into squares.

Makes about 12 brownies

Butterscotch Blondies

¾ cup (1½ sticks) butter or margarine,
   softened
¾ cup packed light brown sugar
½ cup granulated sugar
2 eggs
2 cups all-purpose flour
1 teaspoon baking soda
½ teaspoon salt
1⅔ cups (10-ounce package) HERSHEY'S
   Butterscotch Chips
1 cup chopped nuts (optional)

Heat oven to 350°F. Grease 13×9×2-inch baking pan.
In large bowl, beat butter, brown sugar and granulated
sugar until creamy. Add eggs; beat well. Stir together
flour, baking soda and salt; gradually add to butter
mixture, blending well. Stir in butterscotch chips and
nuts, if desired. Spread into prepared pan. Bake 30 to
35 minutes or until top is golden brown and center is
set. Cool completely in pan on wire rack. Cut into bars.

Makes about 36 bars

Blonde Brickle Brownies

1⅓ cups all-purpose flour
½ teaspoon baking powder
¼ teaspoon salt
2 eggs
½ cup granulated sugar
½ cup packed brown sugar
⅓ cup butter or margarine, melted
1 teaspoon vanilla extract
¼ teaspoon almond extract
1 package (7.5 ounces) BITS 'O BRICKLE®, divided
½ cup chopped pecans (optional)

Preheat oven to 350°F. Grease 8-inch square baking pan. Mix flour, baking powder and salt in small bowl; set aside. Beat eggs in large bowl. Gradually beat in granulated sugar and brown sugar until thick and creamy. Add melted butter, vanilla and almond extract; mix well. Gently stir in flour mixture until moistened. Fold in ⅔ cup BITS 'O BRICKLE® and pecans, if desired. Pour into prepared pan.

Bake 30 minutes. Remove from oven; immediately sprinkle remaining BITS 'O BRICKLE® over top. Cool completely in pan on wire rack. Cut into squares.

Makes about 16 brownies

Decadent Blonde Brownies

1½ cups all-purpose flour
1 teaspoon baking powder
½ teaspoon salt
½ cup butter or margarine, softened
¾ cup granulated sugar
¾ cup packed light brown sugar
2 large eggs
2 teaspoons vanilla extract
1 package (10 ounces) semisweet
  chocolate chunks*
1 jar (3½ ounces) macadamia nuts,
  coarsely chopped

1. Preheat oven to 350°F. Well-grease 13×9-inch baking pan.

2. Combine flour, baking powder and salt in small bowl. Beat butter and sugars in large bowl with electric mixer at medium speed until light and fluffy, scraping down side of bowl once. Beat in eggs and vanilla, scraping down side of bowl once. Add flour mixture. Beat at low speed until well blended, scraping down side of bowl once. Stir in chocolate and nuts with mixing spoon. Spread batter evenly into prepared baking pan.

3. Bake 25 to 30 minutes until golden brown. Remove pan to wire rack; cool completely. Cut into 3¼×1½-inch bars. Store tightly covered at room temperature or freeze up to 3 months.   *Makes 2 dozen brownies*

*If chocolate chunks are not available, cut 10-ounce thick chocolate candy bar into ½-inch pieces to equal 1½ cups.

White Chocolate & Almond Brownies

> 12 ounces white chocolate, broken into pieces
> 1 cup unsalted butter
> 3 eggs
> ¾ cup all-purpose flour
> 1 teaspoon vanilla extract
> ½ cup slivered almonds

1. Preheat oven to 325°F. Grease and flour 9-inch square baking pan.

2. Melt chocolate and butter in large, heavy saucepan over low heat, stirring constantly. Remove from heat when chocolate is just melted. With electric hand mixer, beat in eggs until mixture is smooth. Beat in flour and vanilla. Spread batter evenly in prepared pan. Sprinkle almonds evenly over top.

3. Bake 30 to 35 minutes just until set in center. Cool completely in pan on wire rack. Cut into 2-inch squares. Store tightly covered.

Makes about 16 brownies

White Chocolate Chunk Brownies

4 squares (1 ounce each) unsweetened chocolate, coarsely chopped
½ cup butter or margarine
2 large eggs
1¼ cups sugar
1 teaspoon vanilla extract
½ cup all-purpose flour
½ teaspoon salt
6 ounces white baking bar, cut into ¼-inch pieces
½ cup coarsely chopped walnuts (optional)
   Powdered sugar (optional)

1. Preheat oven to 350°F. Grease 8-inch square baking pan.

2. Melt unsweetened chocolate and butter in small, heavy saucepan over low heat, stirring constantly; set aside.

3. Beat eggs in large bowl with electric mixer at medium speed 30 seconds. Gradually add sugar, beating at medium speed about 4 minutes until very thick and lemon colored. Beat in chocolate mixture and vanilla. Beat in flour and salt at low speed just until blended. Stir in baking bar pieces and walnuts with mixing spoon. Spread batter evenly into prepared pan.

4. Bake 30 minutes or until edges just begin to pull away from sides of pan and center is set. Remove pan to wire rack; cool completely. Cut into 2-inch squares. Place powdered sugar in fine-mesh strainer; sprinkle over brownies, if desired. Store tightly covered at room temperature or freeze up to 3 months.

Makes 16 brownies

Ricotta Cheese Brownies

BROWNIE LAYER
- ½ cup butter or margarine
- ⅓ cup unsweetened cocoa
- 1 cup sugar
- 2 eggs, slightly beaten
- 1 teaspoon vanilla
- ½ cup all-purpose flour
- ½ teaspoon baking powder
- ¼ teaspoon salt

CHEESE LAYER
- ¾ cup (6 ounces) SARGENTO® Part-Skim Ricotta Cheese
- ¼ cup sugar
- 1 egg, slightly beaten
- 2 tablespoons butter or margarine, softened
- 1 tablespoon all-purpose flour
- ½ teaspoon vanilla

For brownie layer: Preheat oven to 350°F. Melt butter in small saucepan; remove from heat. Stir in cocoa; cool. In large bowl of electric mixer, beat sugar, eggs and vanilla on medium speed until light and fluffy. In small bowl, stir together flour, baking powder and salt. Add to egg mixture; beat until blended. Add cocoa mixture; beat until thoroughly combined. Reserve 1 cup batter; spread remaining batter into greased 8-inch square baking pan.

For cheese layer: In small bowl of electric mixer, beat ricotta cheese, sugar, egg, butter, flour and vanilla on medium speed until well blended. Spread over brownie layer in pan. Drop teaspoonfuls of reserved brownie batter over cheese mixture; spread batter with spatula to cover cheese mixture. Bake 40 minutes. Cool.

Makes 16 brownies

PHILLY® Marble Brownies

- 1 package (21½ ounces) brownie mix
- 1 package (8 ounces) PHILADELPHIA BRAND® Cream Cheese, softened
- ⅓ cup sugar
- ½ teaspoon vanilla
- 1 egg
- 1 cup BAKER'S® Semi-Sweet Real Chocolate Chips

PREPARE brownie mix as directed on package. Spread batter in greased 13×9-inch baking pan.

MIX cream cheese, sugar and vanilla with electric mixer on medium speed until well blended. Add egg; mix well. Pour over brownie batter; cut through batter with knife several times for marble effect. Sprinkle with chips.

BAKE at 350°F for 35 to 40 minutes or until cream cheese mixture is lightly browned. Cool in pan on wire rack. Cut into squares. *Makes 2 dozen bars*

The publishers would like to thank the companies and organizations listed below for the use of their recipes and photographs in this publication.

Best Foods, a Division of
 CPC International Inc.
Blue Diamond Growers
California Prune Board
Cherry Marketing Institute,
 Inc.
Diamond Walnut Growers,
 Inc.
Dole Food Company, Inc.
Domino Sugar Corporation
Hershey Foods Corporation
Kahlúa® Liqueur
Kellogg Company
Kraft Foods, Inc.
Leaf®, Inc.
M&M/MARS
MOTT'S® Inc., a division of
 Cadbury Beverages Inc.
Nabisco, Inc.
National Cherry Foundation

Nestlé Food Company
Oregon Washington
 California Pear Bureau
The Procter & Gamble
 Company
The Quaker Oatmeal
 Kitchens
Reckitt & Colman Inc.
Sargento® Foods Inc.
Smucker Company,
 The J.M.
Sokol & Company
Sunkist Growers
The Sugar Association, Inc.
USA Rice Council
Walnut Marketing Board
Washington Apple
 Commission
Wisconsin Milk Marketing
 Board

VOLUME MEASUREMENTS (dry)

⅛ teaspoon = 0.5 mL
¼ teaspoon = 1 mL
½ teaspoon = 2 mL
¾ teaspoon = 4 mL
1 teaspoon = 5 mL
1 tablespoon = 15 mL
2 tablespoons = 30 mL
¼ cup = 60 mL
⅓ cup = 75 mL
½ cup = 125 mL
⅔ cup = 150 mL
¾ cup = 175 mL
1 cup = 250 mL
2 cups = 1 pint = 500 mL
3 cups = 750 mL
4 cups = 1 quart = 1 L

VOLUME MEASUREMENTS (fluid)

1 fluid ounce (2 tablespoons) = 30 mL
4 fluid ounces (½ cup) = 125 mL
8 fluid ounces (1 cup) = 250 mL
12 fluid ounces (1½ cups) = 375 mL
16 fluid ounces (2 cups) = 500 mL

WEIGHTS (mass)

½ ounce = 15 g
1 ounce = 30 g
3 ounces = 90 g
4 ounces = 120 g
8 ounces = 225 g
10 ounces = 285 g
12 ounces = 360 g
16 ounces = 1 pound = 450 g

DIMENSIONS

1/16 inch = 2 mm
⅛ inch = 3 mm
¼ inch = 6 mm
½ inch = 1.5 cm
¾ inch = 2 cm
1 inch = 2.5 cm

OVEN TEMPERATURES

250°F = 120°C
275°F = 140°C
300°F = 150°C
325°F = 160°C
350°F = 180°C
375°F = 190°C
400°F = 200°C
425°F = 220°C
450°F = 230°C

BAKING PAN SIZES

Utensil	Size in Inches/ Quarts	Metric Volume	Size in Centimeters
Baking or Cake Pan (square or rectangular)	8×8×2	2 L	20×20×5
	9×9×2	2.5 L	23×23×5
	12×8×2	3 L	30×20×5
	13×9×2	3.5 L	33×23×5
Loaf Pan	8×4×3	1.5 L	20×10×7
	9×5×3	2 L	23×13×7
Round Layer Cake Pan	8×1½	1.2 L	20×4
	9×1½	1.5 L	23×4
Pie Plate	8×1¼	750 mL	20×3
	9×1¼	1 L	23×3
Baking Dish or Casserole	1 quart	1 L	—
	1½ quart	1.5 L	—
	2 quart	2 L	—